Sensing Space

Technologien
für Architekturen
der Zukunft

Future
Architecture by
Technology

jovis

T0327170

Die Reihe ■:p architektur:positionen wird herausgegeben
von Christiane Fath und Jochen Visscher
The series ■:p architektur:positionen is edited by
Christiane Fath and Jochen Visscher

Umschlag *Cover*: Judith Keller

Bibliografische Information der Deutschen Bibliothek.
Die Deutsche Bibliothek verzeichnet diese
Publikation in der Deutschen Nationalbibliografie;
detaillierte bibliografische Daten sind im Internet über
http://dnb.ddb.de abrufbar.
Bibliographic information published by Die Deutsche
Bibliothek. Die Deutsche Bibliothek lists this
publication in the Deutsche Nationalbibliografie;
detailed bibliographic data are available on the Internet
at http://dnb.ddb.de

Herausgeber *Editors*: plan a / Franziska Eidner,
Nadin Heinich
Konzept und Redaktion *Concept and Editing*:
Franziska Eidner, Nadin Heinich
Redaktionsassistenz *Editing Assistant*:
Eva-Maria Färber
Übersetzung *Translation*: Benjamin Waters
Künstlerische Leitung *Art Director*: Judith Keller
Gestaltung und Satz *Design and Setting*:
Tilman Dominka, Judith Keller
Reinzeichnung *Fine-drawing*: Simon Adrian
Druck und Bindung *Printing and binding*:
GCC Grafisches Centrum Cuno, Calbe

jovis Verlag GmbH
Kurfürstenstraße 15/16
10785 Berlin

www.jovis.de

ISBN 978-3-939633-95-2

Sensing Space wird unterstützt durch
Sensing Space is supported by

Sensing Space ist ein Projekt von
Sensing Space is a project by

Nadin Heinich
Franziska Eidner
Sensing Space

Technologien für Architekturen der Zukunft /

Future Architecture by Technology

α:p architektur:positionen

jovis

Inhalt Content

Sensing Space
Einleitung
Introduction

… ein Bürogebäude, dessen Fassade sich nachts, wenn alle Räume menschenleer sind, in ein sanft pulsierendes Farbspiel verwandelt

… eine Wohnung, die sich über zwei weit entfernte Orte erstreckt und die uns spüren lässt, wenn der Liebste am anderen Ende der Welt nach Hause kommt

… ein Haus, das uns nicht von der Außenwelt abschirmt, sondern uns mit den Geräuschen von „draußen" einen eigenen Soundtrack im Innenen zusammenstellen lässt

Der Titel dieses Buches „Sensing Space" wirft zunächst einmal Fragen auf. Geht es um den wahrnehmenden Raum oder unsere Wahrnehmung von Raum? Architektur und gebaute, gestaltete Umwelt als Sensor oder als unsere Sinne stimulierende Umgebungen? Könnte gar „sensing" im Sinne einer sinnlicheren, uns emotional berührenden Architektur gemeint sein? Die Antwort lautet ja – auf alle der vorangestellten Fragen. Ja, und dies alles im Hinblick auf

… an office building whose façade changes at night, when all of the rooms are empty, into a gently pulsating play of colors.

… an apartment that extends across two far distant locations and lets us know when our loved one is coming home on the other side of the world

… a house that doesn't shield us from the outside world, but rather allows us to put together our own soundtrack in the house with sounds from "outside"

The title of this book "Sensing Space" calls to mind first of all questions. Is it about space that can perceive, or about our perception of space? Architecture and the built, formed environment as sensor, or as surroundings that stimulate our senses? Could "sensing" even be understood in the sense of a sensitive architecture that touches us emotionally? The answer is yes—to all of these questions. Yes, and this in regard to

Technologie als integrativer, gestaltbildender Bestandteil von Architektur. Es geht also nicht um das Entwerfen mithilfe immer ausgeklügelterer Computerprogramme oder um technische Spielereien, die als hippe Accessoires einer Clublounge oder als Display in einem Showroom sich selbst genügen.

Die Fragestellung, die als Grundmotivation hinter diesem Buch steht, mag zunächst naiv klingen. Sie lautet schlicht: Inwiefern können durch die bewusste Integration neuer Technologien Räume entstehen, die uns bewegen und die uns im besten Fall ein Stück weit mehr „zu Hause" fühlen lassen? Daraus ergeben sich weitere (naive?) Fragen: Kann Technologie als integrativer Bestandteil von Architektur angemessene Antworten auf die veränderten Bedürfnisse einer mobilen und global vernetzten Gesellschaft sein? Wie könnten diese Antworten aussehen? Was meint „Zuhause" im 21. Jahrhundert? Was verbirgt sich hinter Begriffen wie „interaktive Räume" oder „intelligente Architekturen"? Dieses Buch ist aus Neugier entstanden – keine Fachliteratur für Spezialisten, sondern für alle, die genauso neugierig auf dieses Thema sind. Eine Art Skizzenbuch, das Collagen sammelt und Ansätze vorstellt, die uns überrascht, inspiriert und zur weiteren Auseinandersetzung angeregt haben.

Bereits 1960 sprach sich der Architekturtheoretiker Reyner Banham für eine offensive Auseinandersetzung mit Technologie aus:

Es ist durchaus möglich, dass das, was wir bisher als Architektur angesehen haben, und das, was wir beginnen, unter Technologie zu

technology as an integrative, formative element of architecture. It is not a matter of architecture designed with increasingly clever computer programs, or of technical tricks that are content to be hip accessories for a club lounge or displays in a showroom.

The question that forms the basic motivation of this book may sound at first naive. It is simply: To what extent can the deliberate integration of new technologies create spaces that move us and in the best case allow us to feel more "at home"? This throws up further (naive?) questions: Can technology as an integrative element provide appropriate solutions to the new needs of a mobile and globally-connected society? What would these solutions look like? What does home mean in the 21st century? What is behind such concepts as "interactive spaces" or "intelligent architectures"? This book is the product of curiosity—it is not technical literature for specialists, but is rather for all those who share our curiosity for this subject. A kind of sketchbook, that collects collages and presents approaches that surprised or inspired us, and stimulated us to further engagement ...

As early as 1960, the architecture theorist Reyner Banham spoke of an offensive contestation with technology:

It is entirely possible that what we have until now understood as architecture and what we are beginning to understand as technology are incompatible disciplines. The architect who intends to move with technology knows that he finds himself in a movement that is quickly

verstehen, miteinander unvereinbare Diszi-
plinen sind. Der Architekt, der beabsichtigt,
mit der Technologie zu gehen, weiß, dass er
sich in einer rasch voranschreitenden Bewe-
gung befindet und dass er, um mit ihr Schritt
zu halten, es möglicherweise den Futuristen
gleichtun und seinen ganzen Kulturballast
abwerfen muss, einschließlich jener Berufs-
kleidung, die ihn als Architekt kenntlich macht.
Wenn er sich andererseits entschließt, das
nicht zu tun, dann wird er vielleicht feststellen,
dass die technologische Kultur entschlossen
ist, ohne ihn voranzuschreiten.[1]

Das Centre Pompidou, 1977 in Paris eröffnet, war dann eines der ersten Gebäude, bei dem die Gebäudetechnik nicht versteckt, sondern auch auf ästhetischer Ebene zum Gegenstand der Auseinandersetzung wurde: Sämtlich Rohre und Leitungskanäle wurden in die Außen-fassade verlegt und farbig gekennzeichnet – Wasserrohre grün, die Stromversorgung gelb und die Rohre der Klimaanlage blau. Neben den Anlagen zur Beheizung, Kühlung, Belüftung und Beleuchtung von Gebäuden bilden aber auch Unterhaltungs- und Kommunikationstech-nologien, Zutrittskontrolle oder Überwachungs-systeme zunehmend wichtigere Bereiche der Gebäudetechnologie. Durch Digitalisierung, die Verbreitung des Internets, Miniaturisierung von Computerprozessen, drahtlose Technologien oder Fortschritte bei der Spracherkennung und Biometrie, die zum Beispiel die Identifizie-rung von Personen durch Netzhautscans oder anhand des Fingerabdrucks ermöglicht, werden immer mehr der in Gebäuden ablaufenden Prozesse automatisiert und untereinander ver-netzt. Ein Leitbild für diese Entwicklung – das

striding ahead, and that in order to keep up he
may have to copy the futurists and throw off
his entire cultural ballast, including the uniform
that identifies him as architect. If he decides, on
the the hand, not to do this, he may perhaps
discover that the technological culture has
decided to move on without him.[1]

The Centre Pompidou, which opened in Paris in 1977, was at that time one of the first buildings in which the building services were not hidden, but rather made an object of examination on an aesthetic level: all of the pipes and ducting systems were set into the exterior façade and marked with a color system—water pipes in green, the electricity supply in yellow, and the ducts of the air conditioning in blue. Beyond systems for the heating, cooling, ventilation and lighting of buildings, entertainment and communication technologies, access control and surveilance systems are becoming ever more important areas in building technology. Through digitalization, the propagation of the internet, the miniaturization of computer processors, wireless technologies and advances in speech recognition and biometrics that make it possible for example to identify people with iris or fingerprint scans, ever more of the processes that occur in buildings are being automated and networked together. One model for this development—that of "ubiquitous computing"— was presented in 1991 by the American com-puter theorist Mark Weiser in his essay "The Computer for the 21st Century": The computer as individual device is to become superfluous, and in its place all of our surrounding everyday objects will be fitted out with digital technol-

des „Ubiquitous Computing" – prägte 1991 der amerikanische Computerforscher Mark Weiser mit seinem Aufsatz „The Computer for the 21st Century": Der Computer wird als Einzelgerät überflüssig, stattdessen werden sämtliche uns umgebende Alltagsgegenstände durch digitale Technologien aufgewertet. Immer kleinere Computer werden – so Weisers Prognose – uns bei all unseren alltäglichen Tätigkeiten unmerklich unterstützen. Doch welche Auswirkungen haben diese und andere technologische Entwicklungen auf die Architektur? Werden wir unsere Wohnungen mit immer mehr elektronischen Einzelobjekten „aufrüsten", „from ‚intelligent' toasters to iPods"[2] ? Bleiben die integrierten Technologien unsichtbar, wie es bei vielen der sogenannten „Smart Homes" der Fall ist – oder können sie auch zu einem Gestaltungsmittel der Architektur werden? Fühlen sich Architekten für diese Fragen überhaupt verantwortlich oder bleiben die verschiedenen Bereiche der (Gebäude-)Technik einzelnen Fachplanern überlassen?

Stehen wir gar vor einer „Dynamisierung der Architektur", wie es Tim und Jan Edler formulieren, die mit ihrem Büro realities:united an der Schnittstelle von Architektur, Technologie und Kunst arbeiten? *Durch eine „mediale" Inanspruchnahme der vernetzten und ertüchtigten (Gebäude-)Technik erobert die Architektur eine neue Wirkungsebene. (…)*

Diese Entwicklung erzeugt veränderliche Gebäude – veränderlich in ihrem Ausdruck, ihrer Atmosphäre, ihrem Aussehen, aber auch veränderlich in ihrem Standort und der inneren Organisation.

ogies. Unnoticed by us, ever smaller computers will help us—in Weiser's prognosis—in all of our daily activities. But what impact do these and other technological developments have on architecture? Will we "arm" our apartments with ever more individual electronic devices, "from ‚intelligent' toasters to iPods"?[2] Will the integrated technologies remain invisible, as is the case in many of the so-called "smart homes"—or can they also become a formative design element of architecture? Do architects feel responsible for answering such questions or will the various areas of (building) technology remain the domains of individual planning experts?

Are we perhaps confronting a "dynamization of architecture," as formulated by Tim and Jan Edler, whose office realities:united is working on the interface between architecture, technology and art? *By availing ourselves of the "medial" possibilities of networked and improved (building) technologies, architecture conquers a new level of effect. …*

This development produces changeable buildings—changeable in their expression, their atmosphere, their appearance, but also changeable in their location and inner organization. They will radically change our conception architecture and city.[3]

Or does the future hold for us an *"Ecosystem" of mutually communicating objects, buildings and virtual environments*[4], as Usman Haque predicts? Buildings that exchange information with each other for instance regar-ding their energy use or rate of occupancy and are even capable of "learning" from each other?

Sie werden unsere Vorstellung von Architektur und Stadt radikal ändern.[3]

Oder erwartet uns in Zukunft *ein „Ökosystem" miteinander kommunizierender Objekte, Gebäude und virtueller Umgebungen[4]*, wie es Usman Haque prognostiziert? Gebäude, die sich etwa über ihren Energieverbrauch oder ihren Auslastungsgrad untereinander austauschen und sogar fähig sind, voneinander zu „lernen"?

Sensing Space möchte durch die vorgestellten räumlichen Experimente, Prototypen und Installationen mögliche Entwicklungen hinsichtlich einiger dieser Fragen aufzeigen. Wir nähern uns dem „Sensing Space" auf drei verschiedenen Ebenen. Das erste Kapitel des Buches RE-CONSTRUCTING HOME fokussiert auf das „Zuhause-Sein", im Kapitel PUBLIC (ATMO)SPHERE wird der Blick auf den öffentlichen Raum erweitert und das dritte Kapitel INTERACTIVE FUTURE führt schließlich noch einen Schritt weiter, indem es Ansätze vorstellt, die sich mit im wahrsten Sinne des Wortes interaktiver Architektur auseinandersetzen, bei der die Nutzer selbst „in Aktion" treten und ihre Umwelt mitgestalten können, bis hin zu lernfähigen Architekturen. Jedes Kapitel wird dabei von einem „Klassiker" eingeleitet, von Pionierprojekten, die in gewisser Weise für viele der nachfolgend vorgestellten Arbeiten Wegbereiter waren, Referenz oder auch Anlass zur kritischen Auseinandersetzung. Der Idee des Skizzenbuchs folgend, sind die ausgewählten Projekte assoziativ aneinander gereiht, immer wieder unterbrochen von Zwischentexten, Notizen, die einzelne Fragestellungen auf-

By presenting spatial experiments, prototypes and installations, "Sensing Space" wants to show some of the possible developments that relate to these questions. We approach "Sensing Space" on three different levels. The first chapter, RE-CONSTRUCTING HOME focuses on "being at home"; in the second chapter, in PUBLIC (ATMO)SPHERE we expand our view to public space; finally, the third chapter, INTERACTIVE FUTURE leads a step further by presenting approaches that examine interactive architecture in the truest sense of the term, in which the users themselves are set "in action" and can form their own environment, through to architectures that are capable of learning. Each chapter begins with a "classic," a pioneer project that was in some sense a trailblazer for the following projects, as a reference or as an occasion for critical examination. Following the idea of a sketchbook, the selected projects follow one another in an associative order, interrupted by linking texts and notes that take up and illuminate the individual problems in more detail. And throughout the text we will hear from some of the protagonists themselves—in the form of interview excerpts and quotes. The 36 projects presented here represent a multitude of further approaches that architects, designers, artists, and research institutes are working on around the world. At the end of Chapter III a collection of links makes it possible to pursue information beyond "Sensing Space."

greifen und ausführlicher beleuchten. Dabei kommen einige der vorgestellten Protagonisten auch immer wieder selbst zu Wort – in Form von Interviewausschnitten und Zitaten. Die insgesamt 36 vorgestellten Projekte stehen dabei stellvertretend für eine Vielzahl weiterer Ansätze, an denen Architekten, Designer, Künstler und Forschungsinstitutionen weltweit arbeiten. Am Ende von Kapitel III bietet eine Auswahl von Links die Möglichkeit, sich über Sensing Space hinaus zu informieren.

Re-Constructing Home

[Das Zuhause] ist der Raum, den wir bewohnen und dem wir uns zugehörig fühlen. Dort, wo wir in einer persönlichen Umgebung unbefangen agieren und wo wir uns einen individuellen Ort schaffen, der unseren elementaren Bedürfnissen und Wünschen gerecht wird. (…) [Das Zuhause] wird zu einem Spiegel unseres Selbst, beeinflusst durch Trends, Moden und Lifestyle-Industrie. In einer Gesellschaft, in der sich Dinge schnell ändern, wird das Bedürfnis nach Anpassung wichtig. Im Moment artikulieren sich unsere Selbstdarstellung und -wahrnehmung vor allem in den Objekten, die wir konsumieren und in den statischen Häusern, in denen wir leben. Doch was wäre, wenn der Raum, eine Oberfläche, eine Wand oder ein Möbelstück über eine große Entfernung hinweg kommunizieren könnten? Was, wenn die Fassaden den Grad an Aktivität und Intensität [im Inneren] in die Stadt [nach außen] mitteilen würde? Was, wenn eine Wand Heizung und Kühlung zugleich wäre, abhängig von unserer eigenen Körpertemperatur? Was, wenn sich die

Re-Constructing Home

[Home is] the space that we inhabit and belong to. It is where we engage naturally within our individual environment and where we create our individual space that fulfills our basic needs and desires. … [The home] becomes a mirror of identification and follows the flow in trends, fashion and the lifestyle industry. In a society were things change fast, the need for adaptation becomes important. At present we achieve recognition and communicate our sense of self in the objects that we consume and the static houses that we live in. But what if the space, a surface, a wall or furniture could communicate over a long distance? What if the surface of a building communicated the level of activity and intensity in the city? What if the wall could heat and cool depending on our body heat? What if the pattern on the wall could change shape, form and depth? What if the wall surface was programmed to fade similarly to the baroque wallpaper in once luxurious apartments?[5]

Technology and the home—in this connection one probably thinks above all of the so-called "smart homes." Here, a multitude of communication, media, and security technologies are mostly invisibly integrated into the home, in order to make our everyday existence as "comfortable, secure and simple" as possible: home cinema and mood lighting with the touch of a button, windows that shut automatically in bad weather, or a security system that can if necessary monitor the movements in every room. But these con-

Muster an der Wand in ihren Umrissen und ihrer räumlichen Tiefe verändern könnten? Was, wenn die Oberflächen der Wände so programmiert wären, dass sie verblassen würden, ähnlich barocken Tapeten in ehemals glanzvollen Apartments?[5]

Technologie und Zuhause – dabei denkt man wahrscheinlich am ehesten an sogenannte „Smart Homes" oder „intelligente Wohnkonzepte". Hier werden eine Vielzahl von Kommunikations-, Medien- und Sicherheitstechnologien zumeist unsichtbar in die Wohnung integriert, um dadurch unseren Alltag so „angenehm, sicher und einfach" wie möglich zu gestalten: Heimkino und Stimmungslicht auf Knopfdruck, Fenster, die bei schlechtem Wetter automatisch schließen oder ein Sicherheitssystem, das bei Bedarf die Bewegungen in jedem Zimmer registriert. Diesen Konzepten wurde jedoch auch viel Kritik entgegengebracht: Warum bleibt die Technik meist unsichtbar? Wie schmal ist der Grad zwischen Selbstbestimmung und dem Gefühl, der Technik ausgeliefert zu sein? Und was passiert, wenn der Strom ausfällt? In einem Interview mit plan a beschreibt Benjamin Otto, Geschäftsführer der „Intelligent Group"[6], einem Unternehmen, das unter anderem auf die Technikplanung in Wohngebäuden spezialisiert ist, die Problematik so:

Viele Kunden wünschen sich, dass die Technik nicht sichtbar ist. Reine Technikmodule, wie zum Beispiel ein Videorecorder, werden häufig als störend empfunden. Daher versuchen wir diese Geräte möglichst formschön und unsichtbar in die Architektur zu integrieren. (…) Außerdem achten wir

ceptions have been widely criticized: Why is the technology mostly invisible? How narrow is the gap between self-control and the feeling of being at the mercy of technology? And what happens when the power cuts out? In an interview with plan a, Benjamin Otto, director of the "Intelligent Group"[6], a business that specializes in, among other things, technology planning in residential buildings, described the problem as follows:

Many clients want the technology to be invisible. Pure technology modules such as video recorders are often considered objectionable. We thus try to integrate these devices into the architecture in the shapeliest and most invisible manner. … We also take great care that even in a total shut down of the system—which occurs these days extremely rarely—the important functions can be activated manually. Electric doors for example have battery backup, or they unlock themselves, so that they can be opened by hand. … A critical point is that the client doesn't want to be directed by some foreign agent. They want to decide for themselves when they want to let the technology do their work for them. Many people also have the fear that the technology will get the upper hand and that particular functions will be automatically activated, without being under our control. I see it here as our task, that of the industry—to make technology always available, but to only employ it when it is wanted and not experienced as an interference.[7]

sehr darauf, dass selbst bei einem Totalaus-
fall des Systems – was heutzutage wirklich
extrem selten vorkommt – die entscheidenden
Funktionen manuell ausgelöst werden können.
Elektrische Türen sind zum Beispiel batterie-
gepuffert bzw. entriegeln sich, damit sie von
Hand geöffnet werden können. (…)

Ein ganz entscheidender Punkt ist, dass
der Kunde nicht fremdbestimmt werden will.
Er möchte selbst entscheiden, wann er die
Technik für sich arbeiten lässt. Auch haben
viele Menschen Angst, dass die Technik über-
hand nimmt und gewisse Funktionen automatisch ausgelöst werden, ohne dass man das
kontrollieren könnte. Hierin sehe ich auch die
Aufgabe der Industrie – die Technik jederzeit
verfügbar zu machen, sie aber nur dann einzu-
setzen, wenn das auch gewünscht und nicht
als störend empfunden wird.[7]

Aber kann Technologie im privaten Wohnraum nicht mehr, als uns – möglichst unsichtbar
und reibungslos funktionierend – den Alltag
(vermeintlich) angenehmer zu gestalten? Wie
individuell kann etwa ein „Mood-Management-
Programm" tatsächlich sein, mit dem wir –
je nach Stimmung – unser Haus entsprechend
audiovisuell bespielen? Diese Begrenztheit,
vielleicht sogar Bevormundung, wird unter anderem in den spielerisch-kritischen Gegenent-
würfen Scattered House und Reconfigurable
House von Adam Somlai-Fischer und Usman
Haque (siehe S. 26) thematisiert.

Wäre es zum Beispiel möglich, ein Zuhause
zu schaffen, dessen (technologische) Anwendungen und Funktionen jederzeit von den

But can technology in private living space
not do more than just—in a maximally invisible
and smoothly functioning way—make our
daily life (putatively) more comfortable? How
individual, for instance, is a "mood management
program," with which we create an appropriate
audio-visual configuration in our house to suit
our mood? This limitedness, perhaps even
dictating to us, is thematized in, among others,
the playful-critical alternative conceptions
Scattered House and Reconfigurable House
of Adam Somlai-Fischer and Usman Haque
(see p. 26).

Would it be possible, for example, to create
a home whose (technological) applications and
functions could be continually changed by the
occupants and adjusted to new needs?

Can the home still be defined as a fixed
place? What is the influence of increasing
mobility, the soaring number of long-distance
relationships and single-occupant households?
What if two geographically distant places
could be "emotionally" connected with each
other, as proposed by Tobi Schneidler with
his installation Remote Home (see p.42)? Or
are "socially-intelligent design objects", like
Schneidler's Lonely Home Bench the better
solution for stressed-out big city singles?
Will robots that continually fret for our attention and devotion become our new "electronic
flatmates", as in the Technological Dream
Series of Dunne & Raby (see p. 52)?

Doesn't being at home also mean
"appropriating" a space, leaving traces? What
if we could "write ourselves into" a space,

Bewohnern geändert und neuen Bedürfnissen angepasst werden können?

Kann das Zuhause überhaupt noch als ein fixer Ort definiert werden? Welchen Einfluss haben die zunehmende räumliche Mobilität, die steigende Zahl von Fernbeziehungen und Single-Haushalten? Was wäre, wenn zwei geografisch getrennte Orte „emotiona" miteinander verbunden werden könnten, wie es Tobi Schneidler mit seiner Installation Remote Home (siehe S. 38) vorschlägt? Oder sind „sozial-intelligente Designobjekte," wie Schneidlers Lonely Home Bench die bessere Lösung für gestresste Großstadtsingles? Werden gar Roboter, die permanent um unsere Aufmerksamkeit und Zuwendung quengeln, zu unseren neuen „elektronischen" Mitbewohnern, so wie in der Technological Dream Series von Dunne & Raby (siehe S. 52)?

Bedeutet Zuhause-Sein nicht auch, sich einen Raum „anzueignen", Spuren zu hinterlassen? Was wäre, wenn wir uns in einen Raum „einschreiben", wenn unsere Berührungen an Wänden und auf Möbeln einen Moment länger sichtbar bleiben würden, wie bei der Installation Housewarming MyHome von J. Mayer H (siehe S. 46)? Wenn Innen- und Außenraum nicht nur visuell, sondern auch auditiv erfahrbar und verborgene Töne zum Klingen gebracht werden könnten? Das Zuhause, mit immer mehr drahtlosen Technologien aufgerüstet – brauchen wir am Ende schließlich einen Schutzraum vor diversen unsichtbaren Strahlungen, eine Art Faradayschen Käfig (siehe S. 58)?

if touching the walls and furniture would remain visible for a moment longer, as in the installation House-warming MyHome by J. Mayer H (see p. 46)? If interior and exterior spaces were not only visually, but also audibly experienceable and unheard sounds were made audible? The home—will we ultimately need a protective space against the various invisible radio waves, a kind of Faraday Cage (see p. 58)?

Public (Atmo)Sphere

The question of overstimulation is relevant not only in private but also in public space. The conjunction of technology and architecture is perhaps most apparent in media façades. That they can be more than just a "toy" for the advertising industry, "littering" the city space with moving pictures as well, is shown by some of the projects presented in chapter II. What are the possible new communication potentials for architecture here? How can a medial façade installation be more than just a megadisplay arbitrarily "stuck on" the front of a building? What kinds of information—beyond advertising—can a building transmit into the city space? And how does this change our perception of the city? Do we not need to develop an "aesthetic of behavior" for medial surfaces, as demanded by realities:united? What is the role of scale, picture resolution, or spatial depth, when they are conceived on an architectural scale?

And what if the façade itself becomes a transmitter of information—a "shop window" for a virtual library that is open to everyone, *as* proposed by the New York office G TECTS

Public (Atmo)Sphere

Die Frage der Überreizung stellt sich nicht nur im privaten, sondern auch im öffentlichen Raum. Am offensichtlichsten wird die Verbindung von Technologie und Architektur vielleicht an den Medienfassaden. Das sie mehr sein können als ein „Spielzeug" der Werbewirtschaft, das den Stadtraum nun auch noch mit bewegten Bildern optisch „zumüllt", zeigen einige der im Kapitel II vorgestellten Projekte. Welche neuen Kommunikationspotenziale für die Architektur sind damit möglicherweise verbunden? Wie können mediale Fassadeninstallationen mehr sein als ein Megadisplay, das willkürlich vor ein Haus „geklebt" wird? Was für Mitteilungen – jenseits von Werbung – könnte ein Gebäude überhaupt in den Stadtraum senden? Und wie verändert sich dadurch unsere Wahrnehmung zur Stadt? Muss nicht erst eine „Ästhetik des Verhaltens" von medialen Oberflächen entwickelt werden, wie es realities:united fordern? Welche Rolle spielen dabei Maßstab, Bildauflösung oder räumliche Tiefe, wenn sie im architektonischen Maßstab gedacht werden?

Und was wäre, wenn die Fassade selbst zum Informationsträger wird – „Schaufenster" einer virtuellen Bibliothek, die für jedermann frei zugänglich ist, wie es das New Yorker Büro G TECTS mit Harlem Mediatech (siehe S. 78) vorschlägt? Oder wenn Häuserfassaden zu Seismografen unserer emotionalen Befindlichkeit würden, wie in dem Projekt Emotional Cities von Erik Kirkortz (siehe S. 90)?

with Harlem Mediatech (see p. 78)? Or if house façades become seismographs of our emotional states, as in the project Emotional Cities by Erik Kirkortz (see p. 90)?

Technology can perhaps also contribute to helping us feel more "at home" in public space, above all in the context of urban anonymity. It can make the invisible visible, open up our environment by bringing to light what was until now imperceptible, and motivate in toward a new, for instance environ-mentally conscious pattern of behavior, as with the green cloud by HeHe (see p. 106). On the other hand, we confront again and again the surveillance scenario of big brother – where technology in public space makes possible more communication and interaction, it also brings with it the danger of increased control by others. Here one would point to Christian Moeller's comical robot sculptures Mojo and Nosy (see p. 96), which playfully make plain the presence of surveillance technologies.

Interactive Future

Chapter III ends "Sensing Space"—here we deal with considerations of the fundamental questions; in some sense the fundamental research in the area of interactive architecture. A "sensing space" in the truest sense of the term, a perceiving space, as an ever newly self-defining organism, capable of learning and continually surprising us, appears (at the moment) utopian. But what exactly is meant by interactivity, a concept defined in architecture by pioneers like Cedric Price, and whose further development and translation into spatial

Technologie könnte möglicherweise dazu beitragen, dass wir uns auch im öffentlichen Raum, vor allem in der urbanen Anonymität, ein Stück weit mehr „zu Hause" fühlen. Sie könnte Unsichtbares sichtbar machen, uns unsere Umgebung durch bisher nicht Wahrnehmbares neu erschließen und uns vielleicht auch zu neuen, etwa umweltbewussteren Verhaltens- weisen motivieren, wie die grüne Wolke von HeHe (siehe S.106). Andererseits drängt sich auch immer wieder das Überwachungsszenario des „Großen Bruders" auf – wo Technologie im öffentlichen Raum mehr Kommunikation und Interaktion ermöglicht, birgt sie ebenso die Ge- fahr zunehmender fremdbestimmter Kontrolle. Exemplarisch sei hier auf Christian Moellers comichafte Roboterskulpturen Mojo und Nosy verwiesen (siehe S. 96), die uns die Präsenz von Überwachungstechnologien spielerisch vor Augen führen.

Interactive Future

Kapitel III beschließt Sensing Space – hier geht es um die Betrachtung ganz grundsätz- licher Fragen, in gewisser Weise um Grund- lagenforschung auf dem Gebiet interaktiver Architekturen. Ein im wahrsten Sinne des Wortes „Sensing Space", ein wahrnehmender Raum, als ein sich ständig neu definierender Organismus, der in der Lage ist, zu lernen und uns immer wieder zu überraschen, scheint (noch) utopisch. Aber was genau bedeutet Interaktivität – ein Begriff, der in der Architektur durch Pioniere wie Cedric Price geprägt wurde und an dessen Fortschreibung bzw. räumlichen Übersetzungsmöglichkeiten nun – mit allen zur Verfügung stehenden Mitteln der Technologie –

possibilities is currently being researched with all available technological means? INTERACTIVE FUTURE gives no final answer, but presents positions that intensively explore the creation of genuinely interactive spaces and "adaptive" architectures—from the "behaving architectures" of the Center for Information Technology and Architecture (see p.126) to the responsive space installations of Ruari Glynn (see p. 132). For Usman Haque, finally, in projects like Pachube (see p. 138) it is decisively about the question of participation—the possibilities of an interactive formation of the environment for a maximal number of people, rather than for an elite minority.

Even if for many of the presented projects concrete applications in architecture, city plan- ning or the design of living spaces would seem to be still in the distant future, we find these projects both noteworthy and necessary in con- nection with the consideration of an " archi- tecture of the future." plan a aims not just to present young protagonists in architecture and city culture, but to force a broader understanding of architecture and design of the environment and to provide a platform for forward-looking positions and interdisciplinary exchange.

We would like to thank all the authors of the projects, who made available information on their work and often also took time to answer our (naive) questions. We thank above all Ruari Glynn, Usman Haque, Adam Somlai- Fischer, Carole Colett, Mette Ramsgard Thomsen, Gordon Kipping, and Tobi Schneidler.

geforscht wird? INTERACTIVE FUTURE liefert dazu keine abschließende Antwort, stellt aber Positionen vor, die sich intensiv mit der Schaffung tatsächlich interaktiver Räume und „lernfähiger" Architekturen auseinandersetzen – von den Behaving Architectures des Center for Information Technology and Architecture (siehe S. 126) bis hin zu den responsiven Rauminstallationen von Ruari Glynn (siehe S.132). Bei Usman Haque geht es schließlich bei Projekten wie Pachube (siehe S. 138) dezidiert um die Frage der Teilhaberschaft – die Möglichkeiten einer interaktiven Umweltgestaltung für möglichst viele Menschen und nicht nur eine elitäre Minderheit.

Auch wenn für viele der vorgestellten Projekte konkrete Anwendungen in der Architektur, Stadtplanung oder Wohnraumgestaltung noch in weiter Ferne scheinen, so halten wir sie, gerade in Bezug auf eine Betrachtung der „Architektur der Zukunft", für beachtenswert und notwendig. Es ist das Ziel von plan a, nicht nur junge Protagonisten in Architektur und Stadtkultur vorzustellen, sondern vor allem auch ein erweitertes Verständnis von Architektur und Umweltgestaltung zu forcieren und eine Plattform für zukunftsweisende Positionen und den interdisziplinären Austausch zu bieten.

Unser Dank gilt vor allem den Projektautoren, die uns Informationen zu ihren Arbeiten zur Verfügung gestellt haben und die sich oftmals noch zusätzlich Zeit für die Beantwortung unserer Fragen genommen haben, insbesondere Ruari Glynn, Usman Haque, Adam Somlai-Fischer, Carole Colett, Mette Ramsgard Thomsen, Gordon Kipping und Tobi Schneidler.

The short descriptions of the projects do perhaps only partial justice to their works— further information can be found by way of the internet addresses in the appendix.

Thanks also go to Judith Keller and Tilman Dominka, without whose design creativity the idea of a sketchbook could not have been realized.

We also thank our corporate partners Dornbracht, Erco and Miele, whose financial support made this project possible, and all of those who encouraged and supported us in "Sensing Space".

Franziska Eidner, Nadin Heinich

Die Kurzbeschreibungen der Projekte werden dabei möglicherweise ihren Arbeiten nur zu einem Bruchteil gerecht – weitere Informationen bieten die im Anhang veröffentlichten Internetadressen.

Dank gilt auch Judith Keller und Tilman Dominka, ohne deren gestalterische Kreativität die Idee des Skizzenbuches nicht realisierbar gewesen wäre.

Wir danken außerdem unseren Unternehmenspartnern Dornbracht, Erco und Miele, die durch ihre finanzielle Unterstützung dieses Vorhaben erst möglich gemacht haben und allen, die uns zu Sensing Space ermutigt und immer wieder darin bestärkt haben.

Franziska Eidner, Nadin Heinich

1 Reyner Banham : Funktionalismus und Technologie, in: Gerd de Bruyn / Stephan Trüby (Hrsg. / eds.), architekturtheorie.doc: Texte seit 1960, Birkhäuser, 2003, S.130. Erstmals veröffentlicht in / Originally published in: Reyner Banham: Theory and Design in the First Machine Age, The Architectural Press, London 1960.

2 Anthony Dunne: www.mitpress.mit.edu/catalog/item/default.asp?ttype=2&tid=1077

3 Auszug aus einem unveröffentlichten Thesenpapier, das realities:united anlässlich ihrer Publikation „Featuring" (Arbeitstitel) verfasst haben. / Excerpt from an unpublished thesis paper written by realities:united for the publication of "Featuring" (working title). (Version: 19.01.2009)

4 Usman Haque in einem Interview mit / in an interview with Tish Shute: www.ugotrade.com/2009/01/28/pachube-patching-the-planet-interview-with-usman-haque/

5 Aus einem unveröffentlichten Thesenpapier von Karen Gamborg, 2007. Die junge dänische Architektin forscht unter anderem über die Idee des „Zuhause" und die raumbildenden Potenziale neuer Textilien für den Wohnbereich. / From an unpublished thesis paper by Karen Gamborg, 2007. The young Danish architect researches among other things the idea of "Home" and the space-forming potential of new textiles for the home environment.

6 2003/04 hat das Unternehmen in Berlin zum Beispiel eine Musterwohnung mit 190 schaltbaren Geräten auf 130 m^2 Wohnfläche entwickelt. Weitere Informationen unter www.intelligent-group.com / The venture developed in 2003/04 in Berlin for example a prototype apartment with 190 switchable devices in 130 m^2 of living space. More informationen at www.intelligent-group.com

7 Interview Otto Benjamin mit / with plan a, 23.03.2009

I.
RE-CONSTRUCTING
HOME

Entfremdung oder Behausung durch Technologie? Alienation or Accomodation with Technology?

Ist „Zu-Hause-Sein" zuerst ein Gefühl – zum Beispiel von Geborgenheit, Sicherheit, Vertrautheit – oder ein klar abgrenzbarer physischer Ort? Wie können im Zeitalter zunehmender (sozialer) Mobilität, von Fernbeziehungen und Single-Dasein adäquate Formen von Zuhause geschaffen werden? Wie kann die Gegenwart eines uns nahe stehenden Menschen für uns spürbar werden, auch wenn sich diese Person an einem weit entfernten Ort befindet? Bietet die Integration neuer Technologien in Architektur dafür eine Lösung?

Wird unser Zuhause immer mehr zu einem „sicheren Kokon", in den wir uns zurückziehen? Oder weichen die Grenzen zwischen Innen- und Außenraum auf? Entwickeln vielleicht sogar die uns umgebenden Alltagsgegenstände ein (geheimes) Eigenleben?

Wollen wir in hochtechnisierten Smart Homes bequemer und sicherer, aber vielleicht auch kontrollierter leben oder uns unser Haus der Zukunft selbst programmieren? Oder müssen wir uns am Ende gar Schutzräume vor der zunehmenden elektromagnetischen Strahlung schaffen?

RE-CONSTRUCTING HOME stellt Visionen und Konzepte des „Zu-Hause-Seins" vor, bei denen sich die Frage nach Entfremdung oder Behausung durch Technologie immer wieder neu stellt.

Is "being at home" more a feeling—of safety, security, familiarity, for example—or a clearly delimitable physical place? How can adequate forms of being at home be produced in a time of increasing (social) mobility, of long-distance relationships and single existence? How can we make the presence of someone close to us felt, even when they are in a far distant place? Does the integration of new technologies into architecture offer a solution?

Are our homes increasingly becoming "safe cocoons" that we retract into? Or are the boundaries between interior and exterior space becoming blurred? Are the everyday objects around us perhaps developing a (secret) life of their own?

Do we just want to live more comfortably and safely in our highly technologized Smart Homes, or perhaps also with more control, programming our house of the future ourselves? Or will we ultimately have to build rooms to protect us against increasing electromagnetic emissions?

RE-CONSTRUCTING HOME presents visions and conceptions of "being at home," in which the question of technology's alienating or accomodating is continually raised anew.

01
Smart Home

TRON / Ken Sakamura (JP) / 1989

technology

behind the
scenes

PAPI ist der Nachfolger des ersten TRON-Hauses und wurde 2004 in der Präfektur Aichi in Japan errichtet.
PAPI, the successor to the first TRON-House, was constructed in 2004 in the Aichi prefecture of Japan.

Mehr als 1000 Computer und Sensoren auf 200 Quadratmetern: Sämtliche Komponenten des **TRON-Hauses**, Fußböden, Wände, Decken, Lichtsteuerung, Klimaanlage etc., waren mit Computern, Sensoren und Aktoren ausgestattet und miteinander vernetzt. In der Küche sorgten Mikrocomputer dafür, dass dem Essen genau die „richtige" Menge an Gewürzen beigefügt wurde. Die Toilette war in der Lage, eine Harnanalyse durchzuführen und eventuelle Abnormalitäten über ein integriertes digitales Datennetz an eine Klinik weiterzuleiten. Das TRON-Haus war das erste der sogenannten „intelligenten Häuser" und wurde von dem japanischen Informatiker Ken Sakamura entwickelt. Bereits seit 1984 verfolgt er die Vision eines „allumfassenden Computer-Zeitalters" mit dem Leitbild des „ubiquitous computing": Der Computer als Einzelgerät wird abgelöst – sämtliche uns umgebenden Alltagsgegenstände durch digitale Technologien aufgewertet. „Intelligente Objekte" sollen Benutzer und Kontext einer bestimmten Situation erkennen und sich adaptiv verhalten. Das Zukunftsbild von Sakamura reicht noch weiter, bis zu ganzen TRON-Städten, bei denen nicht nur Gebäude, sondern auch Fahrzeuge und Straßen miteinander vernetzt sind.

Over 1000 computers and sensors in 200 square meters: all of the components of the **TRON-House**—floor, walls, ceilings, lighting control, air conditioning, etc.— were fitted with computers and sensors and networked together. In the kitchen, microcomputers ensured that exactly the "right" amount of seasoning was added to the food. The toilet was capable of performing a urine-analysis and relaying information on possible abnormalities to a clinic over an integrated digital network. The TRON-House was the first of the so-called "intelligent houses," and was developed by the Japanese computer scientist Ken Sakamura. As early as 1984 he was already pursuing the vision of an "age of all-encompassing computers," on the model of "ubiquitous computing:" instead of seeing the computer as a piece of stand-alone equipment, all of the everyday objects in our surroundings are enhanced with digital technologies. "Intelligent objects" should recognize the user and the context of a particular situation, and behave adaptively. Sakamura's future vision extends even further, through to entire TRON-cities, where not only buildings, but also vehicles and streets would be networked together.

The residents of **PAPI** carried portable "data stations," so-called "Ubiquitous Communicators" with them. These controlled the lights, air-conditioning, and various other functions in the building. Using RFID-technology, infrared interfaces, and other sensors, these devices were designed to recognize the context of a particular situation and make adjustments to meet the needs of the resident. Different menu options were displayed on the device, appropriate to each situation.

Die Bewohner von **PAPI** führten hier tragbare „Datenstationen", sogenannte „Ubiquitous Communicators" mit sich. Sie dienten dazu, Licht, Klimaanlage sowie verschiedene andere Funktionen im Gebäude zu steuern. Mittels RFID-Technologie, Infrarot-Schnittstellen sowie weiteren Sensoren sollten diese Geräte den Kontext einer bestimmten Situation erkennen und sich den Bedürfnissen der Bewohner anpassen. Entsprechend wurden jeweils unterschiedliche Menüpunkte auf den Geräten angezeigt.

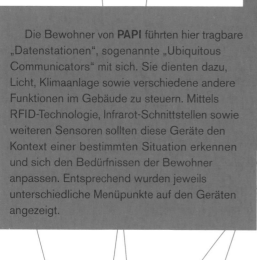

Die Fenster im TRON-Haus wurden durch Computer gesteuert. Die äußeren Wetterverhältnisse, wie Windstärke und Richtung, Temperatur, Regen, wurden mittels Sensoren überwacht. Ein Computersystem entschied dann, ob zum Beispiel die gewünschte Innenraumtemperatur bereits durch das Öffnen der Fenster und ohne Einschalten der Klimaanlage erreicht werden konnte.

The windows in the TRON-house were computer-controlled. The outside weather conditions, such as wind velocity and direction, temperature, and rain were monitored with sensors. A computer system could then decide whether, for example, the desired interior temperature could be achieved simply by opening the windows, without turning on the air conditioning.

02
Fragmented Home

Reconfigurable House / Adam Somlai Fischer (HU), Usman Haque (UK) +
Team (siehe/see Credits, S./p. 160) / 2008
Scattered House / Adam Somlai Fischer (HU), Usman Haque (UK),
Bengt Sjölén (SE) + Team (siehe/see Credits, S./p. 160) / 2008

Während Smart Homes Technologie vor dem Nutzer weitestgehend verstecken, lädt die Installation **Reconfigurable House** dazu ein, diese aktiv zu benutzen. Mit spielerischen Elementen wird Technologie „entsakralisiert". Reconfigurable House setzt auf durch Laien neu „zu verdrahtende" Low-Tech-Bauteile statt auf von Experten programmierte High-Tech-Anwendungen. Im Haus miaut, klingelt, quäkt und flimmert es. Billiges Elektronikspielzeug made in China wird verknüpft mit MP3-Playern, Walkie-Talkies und Laserpointern und so zu interaktiven Objekten umfunktioniert. Die Wände und Geräte des „Hauses" reagieren auf Geräusche, Lichter, Berührungen, Anrufe und können sogar über Remote-Verbindungen von anderen Orten beeinflusst werden. Die (Re-)Aktionsmöglichkeiten des Hauses lassen sich durch eine einfache Bedienoberfläche immer wieder neu bestimmen. Dabei reagiert das Haus nicht nur auf externe Reize, sondern kann sich auch selbst „rekonfigurieren". Sowohl die verwendete Soft- als auch Hardware basieren auf dem Open-Source-Prinzip: Alle Programmiercodes sind frei zugänglich, zusätzliche Geräte können einfach hinzugefügt werden.

Where the Smart Homes hide technology from the user as far as possible, the installation **Reconfigurable House** invites us to actively use it. Technology is "desacralized" with playful elements. Reconfigurable House opts for low-tech components "wireable" by ordinary users, instead of high-tech applications programmed by experts. Inside the house it meows, rings, squawks, and flickers. Cheap electronic toys made in China are connected with MP3-players, walkie-talkies, and laser pointers and thus converted into interactive objects. The walls and devices of the "house" react to sound, light, touch, and telephone calls, and can even be directed by way of remote connections from other places. The (re-)action possibilities of the house can be reconfigured with a simple operating interface. The house not only reacts to external stimuli, but can also "reconfigure" itself. Both the software and the hardware are based on the Open-Source-Principle: all programming code is freely available, additional devices can simply be added.

meow

do it your self !

Reconfigurable House ist eine Weiterentwicklung von Re-Orient (ungarischer Beitrag zur 10. Architekturbiennale Venedig, Abbildung siehe vorherige Seite).
Reconfigurable House is based on Re-Orient (Hungarian contribution to the 10th Architecture Biennale Venice, image see page before).

Scattered House ist eine Weiterentwicklung der Idee des rekonfigurierbaren Hauses. Hier steht nicht nur das ständig veränderbare Haus im Vordergrund, sondern die Idee eines „fragmentierten Zuhauses", das mehrere Orte – virtuelle wie auch physische Räume – miteinander verbindet.

Besucher des Londoner Architekturfestivals – von Studenten bis zu Familien mit Kindern – waren eingeladen, aus mitgebrachten und zur Verfügung gestellten elektronischen Spielzeugen das Scattered House, also ein im wortwörtlichen Sinne „verstreutes" Haus, zu konstruieren. Zusätzlich wurden über den von Usman Haque entwickelten Webservice Pachube (siehe S. 138) Verbindungen zu Orten in Ungarn und Japan hergestellt. Scattered House spiegelt die Idee eines Zuhauses wider, wie sie nach Meinung der Projektautoren schon von vielen von uns gelebt wird. Wir sind an vielen Orten, in verschiedensten Subkulturen (und Webcommunities) beheimatet – „Zuhause ist kein Ort, es ist eine Komposition von Fragmenten", heißt es im Konzepttext zu Scattered House. In der Konsequenz muss sich auch die Architektur selbst fragmentieren.

DRRF

Scattered House is a further development of the idea of a reconfigurable house. The central idea here is not just that of a continually changeable house, but of a "fragmented home" that binds multiple places—virtual as well as physical spaces—together.

Visitors to the London Architecture Festival—from students to families with children—were invited to construct a literally "scattered house" using electronic toys that were provided, or that they had brought along themselves. Additionally, connections to places in Hungary and Japan were established, using the web service Pachube, developed by Usman Haque (see p. 138). Scattered House reflects an idea of home which in the view of the project creators, is already being lived out by many of us. We are at home in many places, in different subcultures (and web-communities). "Home is not a place, but a composition of fragments," claims the concept text to Scattered House. Consequently, architecture will have to fragment itself as well.

Smart?

Vom „intelligenten" Haus zum fragmentierten Zuhause
From "Intelligent" House to Fragmented Home

Mit dem TRON Intelligent House hat der japanische Computerwissenschaftler Ken Sakamura im Jahr 1989 das erste sogenannte Smart Home und mit dem Toyota Dream House PAPI im Jahr 2004 eine Fortsetzung realisiert. 1000 Computer beherbergte das mehr als 7 Millionen Euro teure TRON-Haus auf 200 Quadratmetern Fläche, sichtbar waren sie allerdings kaum. In einem Interview mit plan a beschreibt Ken Sakamura seinen Ansatz so:

Technologie sollte soweit wie möglich versteckt werden. Das haben wir in beiden TRON-Häusern versucht. Im PAPI-Haus wurde etwa ein kleiner, gemütlicher Raum für die Teezeremonie integriert. In dieser traditionellen Umgebung wollten wir keine plumpen LEDs herumflackern lassen. Wir waren so sehr darum bemüht, die Steuerungssysteme zu verbergen, dass ein befreundeter Computerwissenschaftler, der uns im TRON-Haus besuchte, enttäuscht war, kaum sichtbare Zeichen der Computer zu erkennen. In gewisser Weise zeigt seine Reaktion den Erfolg unseres Ansatzes: Wir wollen Häuser bauen, in denen Computer nur notwendige Unterstützung bieten, ohne zu deutlich in Erscheinung zu treten.

In 1989, the Japanese computer scientist Ken Sakamura made the first so-called Smart Home with the TRON Intelligent House; with the Toyota Dream House PAPI in 2004 he has achieved a further development. The more than seven-million-euro TRON-House had 1000 computers in 200 square meters of space, though none can be seen. In an interview with plan a, Ken Sakamura describes his approach:

Technology should be hidden as much as possible if we can afford to. That is what we have done in the two TRON Houses. For example, we built a special small cozy room for traditional Japanese tea ceremony in PAPI. We don't want a clumsy LED flickering in such traditional setting. We tried to hide computers so much in the first TRON House that a visiting computer scientist was disappointed that he could not easily detect any visible trace of computers. In a sense, his reaction showed the success of our approach. We are interested in building houses where computers offer only the necessary help without too much presence.

Dem TRON-Haus folgten weltweit weitere Prototypen intelligenter Häuser, in denen es vor allem um die Präsentation neuer Kommunikations- und Gebäudetechnologien ging. Ob im Orange Future Home (2000), im Philips HomeLab (2003) oder im T-Com-House (2005)[1] – die Verbindung von Architektur und Technologie reicht hier über die – möglichst unsichtbare – Integration von (vermeintlichen) technologischen Annehmlichkeiten im Bereich der Unterhaltungselektronik, automatisierter Hausbeleuchtung oder Raumklimatisierung selten hinaus. Man kann mit seiner Waschmaschine oder seinem Kaffeeautomaten sprechen, den Film auf dem in der Wand integrierten Bildschirm mit einer Liveschaltung ins benachbarte Kinderzimmer unterbrechen oder sich aus der Ferne ein Bad einlassen. Über den Mood Manager kann der Bewohner im T-Com darüber hinaus zwischen fünf voreingestellten Raumszenarien aus Licht, Klang und Bildern wählen: „zum Beispiel ein leises Meeresrauschen aus der Dolby-Surround-HiFi-Anlage, kombiniert mit einem Unterwasserfilm auf einem Multifunktions-Bildschirm im Wohnzimmer, das vollkommen in hellblaues Licht getaucht ist."[2]

Diese „Häuser der Zukunft" stellen dabei kaum den Status Quo des Zuhauses in Frage. In der Verbindung von Architektur und Technologie geht es hier vor allem um die Erhöhung der Annehmlichkeiten, um Sicherheits- und Energiestandards, um die technische Aufrüstung des Hauses zur Unterhaltungs- und Wellness-Oase. Fast scheint es, dass die Entwickler der „Intelligenten Häuser" mehr oder weniger von einem passiven Bewohner ausgehen, dem möglichst viele Tätigkeiten

The TRON-House was followed around the world by further prototypes of intelligent houses, which focused on the presentation of new communication and building technologies. Whether in the Orange Future Home (2000), the Philips HomeLab (2003), or the T-Com-House (2005)[1], the connection between architecture and technology rarely goes beyond the—maximally invisible—integration of (supposed) technological conveniences in the domain of entertainment electronics, automated lighting or air conditioning. One can speak with one's washing machine or coffee machine, interupt the film on the wall-integrated screen with a live picture of the children's room next door, or have the bath filled remotely. With the Mood Manager, the resident in T-Com can choose between five programmed room scenarios using light, sound, and images: "for example a quiet sound of the ocean out of the Dolby-Surround-Hifi-System, combined with an underwater film on the multifunctional screen in the living room, which is bathed in a light blue light."[2]

These "houses of the future" hardly call into question the status quo of the home. Here the connection between architecture and technology is primarily about increasing amenities, security, and energy standards, as well as outfitting the house as an entertainment and wellness oasis. It almost seems as if the developers of the "intelligent houses" presuppose a passive inhabitant, who wants to be disburdened of as many tasks as possible, to be looked after, guarded, and entertained. Architecture offers here the wrapping for applications programmed and predetermined by specialists.

abgenommen, der umsorgt, behütet und unterhalten werden soll. Architektur bietet dabei die Hülle für die von Spezialisten programmierten und damit vorbestimmten Anwendungen.

Junge Architekten und Designer wie der Ungar Adam Somlai-Fischer setzen auf einen anderen, stärker am Individuum orientierten Umgang mit Technologie im Kontext von Raumbildung. plan a sprach mit ihm über eine zeitgenössische Interpretation des „Zuhauses" und eine entschieden menschliche Architektur.

plan a: *Was bedeutet „Zuhause" im 21. Jahrhundert? Was sind die größten Herausforderungen, die sich der Architektur diesbezüglich stellen?*

ASF: *Ich denke, in erster Linie geht es um die Brüchigkeit unserer Vorstellung von „Zuhause". Es ist nicht ein Ort, noch nicht einmal ein Land oder eine Kultur. Selbst ich, der in einer Zeit vor den Online-Communities aufwuchs, fühle mich an vielen Orten und Subkulturen zu Hause: zum Beispiel in Ungarn, in Skandinavien, in der Community von Flash-Entwicklern, die ich im Jahr 2003 kennen gelernt habe, oder unter Spielzeug-Hackern. All diese Bruchstücke meiner Identität haben auch ein Zuhause. Manche davon sind physisch, andere virtuell auf Websites – sie lassen sich schwer einordnen. Wenn sich Architektur mit solchen Identitäten auseinandersetzen soll, dann muss sie sich selbst fragmentieren und immer wieder anpassen.*

Young architects and designers such as the Hungarian Adam Somlai-Fischer set out from a different, more individually oriented relation to technology in the context of designing space. plan a spoke with him about a contemporary interpretation of "home" and a decisively human architecture.

plan a in conversation with Adam Somlai-Fischer on the notion of home and resolutely human architecture

plan a: *What does "home" mean in the twenty-first century? What are the biggest challenges architecture has to deal with in this regard?*

ASF: *I think that foremost it's the fragmentation of our notion of the home. Its not one place, not even one country, not even one culture. Even I, growing up before online communities took off, have the 'home' feeling for many places and subcultures—from Hungary to Scandinavia to flash developers of 2003 or toy hackers. All of these fragments in my identity have a home as well, some physical, some as websites, but they are hard to put into an order. If architecture is to deal with such identities, it will have to fragment itself and adopt over time as well.*

plan a: *So, you would say that the biggest challenge of architecture is not to exclude fragmentation and create a shelter but to integrate it into an open network, a fluid space? Do you think the idea of a stability, of "my home is my castle," has become obsolete at all?*

plan a: *Du würdest also sagen, die größte Herausforderung für die Architektur besteht darin, Fragmentierung nicht zu vermeiden und Schutzräume zu erschaffen, sondern sie in einem offenen Netzwerk, in einem „fließenden" Raum zu integrieren? Hat sich die Idee von Stabilität à la „My home is my castle" über- holt?*

ASF: *Das Schloss stand immer für Stabilität. Heutzutage bietet ein großes, inter- nationales Netzwerk mit verschiedenen Formen von „Zuhause" ein großes Maß an Stabilität. Es handelt sich einfach um die Verschiebung von Werten und Vertrauen.[3] Das Gefühl von Sicherheit und Stabilität von „Zuhause" ist diesen Netzwerken inhärent – je mehr Bestandteile sie in sich vereinen, desto zahlreicher sind die Auswahlmöglichkeiten, die sie für die Zukunft bieten können, und umso weniger verletzbar wird man selbst.*

Ich fühle mich also eher an einem Ort zu Hause, der aus Fragmenten besteht, der kulturelle Codes und Vielfältigkeit in sich aufnimmt, anstatt von Minimalismus und dem Design eines einzelnen Urhebers geprägt zu sein. Er ist offen für Veränderung und zeigt, dass er das Produkt vieler Hände ist. Wir haben dieses Produktionsmodell in unseren Projekten erforscht, in denen wir entweder die allgemeine Öffentlichkeit oder viele Fachleute gleichzeitig involvierten. Scattered House, das ich zusammen mit Usman Haque und Bengt Sjölén für das Architekturfestival 2008 in London realisiert habe, ist ein aktuelles Bei- spiel dafür. Es verdeutlicht zudem die Idee, dass es keinen Unterschied zwischen „virtuell"

ASF: *The castle always stood for stability. A large international network of various "homes" offers a great deal of stability today. It is simply a shift of values and trust.[3] The feeling of safety and stability of the home is present in these networks—the more pieces it is made of, the more choices of future it offers, the less vulnerable one becomes.*

I feel at home in a space that is built up from fragments and collects cultural codes and multiplicity rather than trying to have a minimalist and single-author design. It is open to change and shows that it is the product of many hands. I think we have explored this model of production in these projects, involv- ing either the public or many professionals at a time. They also became "smart," or well networked and responsive, since that was the most natural space we could think of with a flux of people making them. A recent example is Scattered House, which we did with Usman Haque and Bengt Sjölén for the 2008 London Festival of Architecture.

Furthermore, Scattered House emphasizes the idea that there is no distinction between "virtual" and "real" or "local" and "remote"— the distant half of the house, linked via the network is treated equivalently to the "local" half (in both directions) and suggests an un- derstanding of architecture that is resolutely "human" (in the sense of being something that can be inhabited and designed and determined by its occupants) yet context-free (because it does not privilege geographical location).

und „real" oder „lokal" und „entfernt" gibt.
Durch die Verbindung über das Netzwerk ist
die entlegenere Hälfte des Hauses der
„lokalen" Hälfte gleichgestellt. Scattered
House legt ein Verständnis von Architektur
nahe, das entschieden „menschlich" ist –
im Sinne von etwas, das bewohnt, entworfen
und von seinen Bewohnern bestimmt werden
kann – und sich jedoch nicht auf einen be-
stimmten geografischen Ort bezieht.

plan a: Sind Deiner Meinung nach die
so genannten „Smart Homes" oder „intelligen-
ten Häuser", zum Beispiel Projekte wie das
TRON-Haus, geeignete Antworten? Falls
nicht, wieso?

ASF: Intelligenz wird als die „Fähigkeit zu
verstehen" definiert. Strukturen, die einen
Sinn dafür haben, wofür sie genutzt werden
und entsprechend reagieren, könnten also als
intelligent betrachtet werden. Unser kulturelles
Verständnis von Intelligenz geht aber darüber
noch hinaus. Wir erwarten von einem intelli-
genten Objekt, dass es sich auch über die Zeit
anpasst, weiterentwickelt und sogar von selbst
aktiv wird. Und das ist natürlich sehr ambiva-
lent. Man denke an die frustrierten Aufzüge in
Douglas Adams Roman „Das Restaurant am
Ende des Universums", die über Intelligenz
und Präkognition verfügen. Ich glaube, dass
viele dieser sogenannten intelligenten Räume
ebenso frustriert sein würden, wenn sie am
Ende tatsächlich intelligent wären.

Ich sehe das größte Problem der hochtech-
nischen Smart Homes in ihrem Versuch, auch
eine Kultur anzubieten. Diese Kultur wurde

plan a: *Are the so called "Smart homes" or*
"intelligent houses," projects like the TRON
House, appropriate responses in your opinion?
If not, why?

ASF: *Intelligence by definition is the ability*
to comprehend, so structures that have a
sense of what they are being used for, and
respond to that could be considered intelligent.
However, I think our cultural understanding
of intelligence goes beyond that—we expect
an intelligent thing to adapt over time as well,
and even to initiate. And this is really tricky
of course. Think of the frustrated elevators
with intelligence and precognition in Douglas
Adams fiction "The Restaurant at the End of
the Universe"—I often feel that many examples
of intelligent spaces would end up "frustrated"
if they succeeded in making then intelligent.

I think the most problematic aspect of high-
tech smart homes is that they try to offer a
culture as well, one which is nicely caricatured
in "The Sleeper" by Woody Allen. I think our
research offers an alternative to this, but would
not exist without the initial steps to which we
offer the alternative.

plan a: *What is your vision for future de-*
velopments in the field of architecture and
technology?

ASF: *Our digital environment is becoming*
more and more adapted to our identities, we
are increasingly free to build our identities
from larger choices, the built environment will
clearly reflect this. People are simply getting
used to being co-producers in everything.

sehr schön in „Der Schläfer" von Woody Allen karikiert. Ich denke, unsere Projekte bieten dazu Alternativen an, die allerdings ohne die anfänglichen Schritte der Industrie nicht existieren würden.

plan a: Wie sieht Deine persönliche Vision für zukünftige Entwicklungen im Bereich Architektur und Technologie aus?

ASF: Unsere digitale Umgebung passt sich immer mehr unserer individuellen Identität an – wir haben zunehmend größere Auswahlmöglichkeiten, womit wir uns (virtuell) umgeben und auch die gebaute Umgebung wird das eindeutig reflektieren (müssen). Die Menschen werden sich einfach daran gewöhnen, Co-Produzenten in allem zu sein. Man denke nur daran, wie Kinder ihre Zimmer mit Bandpostern „markieren" und sich damit von der Familienidentität separieren. Wir werden möglicherweise noch erleben, wie dies in größerem Maßstab und mit einer größeren Gruppe geschieht, wie sich Architektur immer wieder einer persönlichen Auswahl anpasst, um so individuelle Identität auszudrücken, unabhängig davon, wo man sich gerade befindet. Eine Wendung hin zum Individuum, sogar in Echtzeit – Menschen und Räume als Akteure, die sich austauschen und neue Prozesse initiieren.

A simple example is of this is the way kids mark their rooms with posters of bands— how they separate it from the family image— we might see this happening on larger scale and with larger groups: how architecture will adapt to your choices wherever you are allowing you to express your identity, down to the individual, even real-time. You, surrounded by the status and profile you choose. Maybe this is where a discourse on intelligence might come in—people and their flocking spaces as actors exchanging and initiating.

1 Zur historischen Entwicklung der Smart Homes liefert folgender Beitrag von Jochen Eisenbrand einen ausgezeichneten Überblick / For a good overview of the historical development of Smart Homes, see Jochen Eisenbrand's article Jochen Eisenbrand : „Vom mechanischen Kern zum intelligenten Haus: Zur Beziehung von Architektur und Gebäudetechnik", erschienen in: von Alexander Vegesack / Jochen Eisenbrand: *Open House. Architektur und Technologie für intelligentes Wohnen*, Weil am Rhein 2006, S. / p. 23–53.

2 Aus der Pressemitteilung „Partner für Innovationen", vgl. / From the press release "Partner für Innovationen", see http://www.innovationen-fuer-deutschland.de/pressebuero/pressemitteilungen/detail.php?klasse=16&oid=687

3 Anmerkung von ASF: eine sehr inspirierende Studie über die Verschiebung von Vertrauensstrukturen findet sich bei Michel Bauwen / Note by ASF: a very inspiring study on the displacement of structures of trust can be found in Michel Bauwen (www.p2pfoundation.net http://www.p2pfoundation.net)

03
Remote Home

The RemoteHome / Tobi Schneidler (UK/GER) + Team
(siehe / see Credits, S./p. 160) / 2003

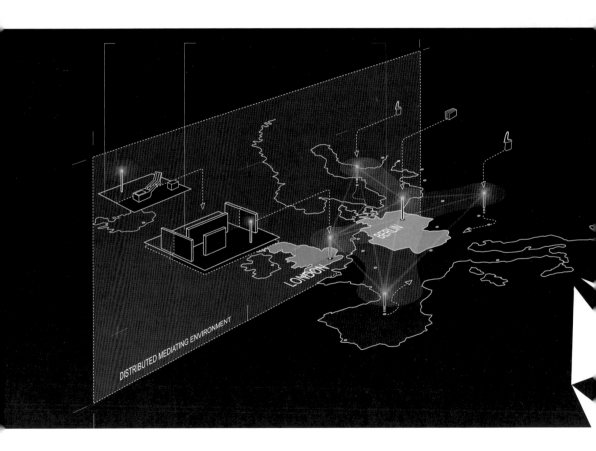

DISTRIBUTED MEDIATING ENVIRONMENT

LONDON

BERLIN

Mittels E-Mail, Mobiltelefon und Skype können heutzutage Verbindungen zum entfernt lebenden Liebsten in (Fast-)Echtzeit aufgebaut, Fernbeziehungen „gemanagt" werden. Was aber ist mit diesen kleinen Spuren der Anwesenheit, die uns erst das Gefühl vermitteln, dass der andere „wirklich da" ist? Das Klicken des Wohnungsschlüssels in der Haustür, Schritte im Hausflur, das zerwühlte Kissen auf dem Sofa … Die Installation **RemoteHome** ist ein Prototyp für eine Wohnung, die sich über zwei verschiedene Orte erstreckt. Sie wurde im Mai 2003 im Science Museum in London und gleichzeitig bei raumlabor in Berlin gezeigt. Das Besondere dabei ist, dass RemoteHome auf die emotionale Interaktion zwischen den sich nahe stehenden, jedoch räumlich entfernt voneinander lebenden Bewohnern fokussiert. Möbel, Wände und Beleuchtung in beiden „Teilen" der Wohnung sind mit Sensoren sowie verschiedenen beweglichen Bauteilen ausgestattet und via Internet miteinander verbunden. Die gesamte Wohnung wird zu einer Art „intuitivem Kommunikationsmittel", das ihren Bewohnern ermöglicht, sich auch über geografische Grenzen hinweg verbunden zu fühlen.

one home in cities

Today we can use email, mobile phones, and **Skype** to establish (almost) real-time contact to loved ones living far away; long distance relationships can be "managed." But what of the small traces of presence that are required to give us the feeling that the other is "really there?" The click of the key in the front door, footsteps in the corridor, the rumpled cushion on the sofa … The installation **RemoteHome** is a prototype for an apartment, that extends across two different locations. It was presented in 2003 at the Science Museum in London and simultaneously at raumlabor in Berlin. What is unique is that RemoteHome focuses on the emotional interaction between occupants who have a close relationship to one another, but are living far apart. Furniture, walls and lighting in both "parts" of the apartment are fitted with sensors and various moveable elements, and are networked together via internet. The entire apartment becomes a kind of "intuitive communication medium," which makes it possible for the occupants to feel connected with one another across geographical limits.

Prinzipskizze des RemoteHome
Scale diagram RemoteHome

emotional con

Ausgelöst durch die Bewegungsabläufe im jeweils anderen Teil der Wohnung geraten die Wandpaneele in Bewegung. Sie wölben sich nach innen und außen und werden so zu einer Art „Pulsmesser" des RemoteHome. Die Paneele sind zudem mit temperaturempfindlicher Farbe beschichtet, deren Farbton sich ändert, je nachdem, ob der Partner zu Hause ist oder nicht.

Activated by sequences of movements in other parts of the apartment, the wall panels are set into motion. By arching in and out they become a kind of "pulse monitor" of the RemoteHome. The panels are also coated with temperature-sensitive paint, which changes its color depending on whether the partner is at home or not.

Durch die „Remote Bag" können die Bewohner auch auf Reisen mit ihrem RemoteHome verbunden bleiben. Vibrations- und Lichtsignale an der Tasche zeigen an, ob gerade jemand zu Hause ist.

With the "Remote Bag" the occupants of the RemoteHome can also stay connected while travelling. Vibration and light signals on the bag show if someone is presently at home.

41

04
Lonely Home

Robotic Furniture: Lonely Home Bench / Tobi Schneidler (GB) / 2005

**Die Lonely-Home-Bank als „Partnerersatz"
für Single-Haushalte: Die Bank entwickelt ein
Eigenleben und „überrascht" den Besitzer
mit unvermittelten Aktionen.**

The Lonely Home Bench as "partner replacement" for single-households: the bench
takes on a life of its own and "surprises" the
owner with sudden actions.

Während das RemoteHome eine Lösung für Menschen in Fernbeziehungen offeriert, bietet das **Lonely Home** ein Szenario für die steigende Zahl von Single-Haushalten. In der Weiterentwicklung der Idee des RemoteHome geht es hier nicht mehr um die emotionale Interaktion zwischen zwei Menschen. Die Verbindung zwischen den Wohnungen wurde mittlerweile gekappt. Aus der „Busy Bench" des Remote Homes, die in Berlin anzeigte, wenn sich jemand in London auf sie setzte (und vice versa) wurde die „Lonely Home Bench". Diese Bank aus der Familie der Robotic Furniture – laut Schneidler ein „sozial intelligentes Designobjekt" – wird nun zu einer Art „Partnerersatz". Der Hybrid aus Möbel und robotischem Haustier – man denke nur an AIBO von Sony, ein Roboterhund für Allergiker – kann unauffällig in die Wohnzimmereinrichtung integriert werden. Doch ganz plötzlich kann die Bank auch zusammenzucken und ihren Be-Sitzer ins Wanken bringen.

While the RemoteHome offers a solution for those with long-distance relationships, the **Lonely Home** is a scenario for the increasing number of single households. This further development of the idea of the RemoteHome is no longer about the emotional interaction between two people. The connection between apartments is now cut off. The "Busy Bench" of the Remote Home, which would give indications in Berlin when someone in London was sitting on it (and vice versa), now becomes the "Lonely Home Bench." This bench, from the family of Robotic Furniture—a "socially intelligent design object" according to Schneidler— becomes a kind of "partner replacement." This hybrid of furniture and robotic pet—one thinks of Sony's AIBO, the robot dog for those with allergies—can be inconspicuously integrated into the living room furnishings. But the bench can suddenly jump into life and give its owner a shake.

05
Poetic Textiles

Toile de Hackney / Carole Collet (UK) / 2005

Poetic Textiles for Smart Homes sind Stoffe, die uns eine Geschichte erzählen. Carole Collet untersucht im Rahmen dieses Forschungsprojektes die Kombination neuer Technologien mit Low-Tech-Methoden für neue „hybride" Textildesigns. Es geht ihr explizit um die Erzeugung eines Gefühls von „Zu-Hause-Sein". **Toile de Hackney** (2005) sind zum Beispiel interaktive Vorhänge, die intelligente Textiltechnologie mit traditionellem Stoffdruck verbinden, inspiriert von den „Toiles de Jouy" aus dem 18. Jahrhundert. Die Stoffe zeigen Alltagsszenen aus dem Londoner Stadtteil Hackney – die romantischen Landschaften der originalen „Toiles de Jouy" werden hier zeitgenössisch interpretiert, zum Beispiel durch eine zugemüllte Parkbank. Die Textilien sind unter anderem mit wärmesensiblen Farben beschichtet und auf einen leitfähigen Stoff laminiert, der so programmiert ist, dass er in regelmäßigen Abständen Wärme produziert. Wenn die Toiles aktiviert sind, verändert sich die Szenerie farblich und enthüllt so versteckte Details – etwa den Müllhaufen unter der Parkbank.

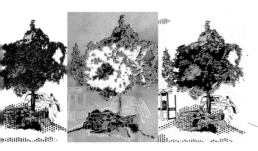

Poetic Textiles for Smart Homes are fabrics that tell a story. In this research project, Carole Collet investigates the combination of new technologies with low-tech methods to create new "hybrid" textile designs. The explicit aim is to create a feeling of "being at home." **Toile de Hackney** (2005) for example are interactive curtains that combine intelligent textile technology with traditional fabric printing, inspired by the "Toiles de Jouy" of the eighteenth century. The fabrics show everyday scenes from the London district of Hackney—the romantic landscapes of the original "Toiles de Jouy" are given a contem-porary inter-pretation, with, for example, a park bench surrounded by rubbish. The textiles have among other things a heatsensitive coating laminated over a conductive material that is programmed to produce heat at regular intervals. When the Toiles are activated, the scenery changes color and unveils hidden details—such as the heap of rubbish under the park bench.

Statt auf kühle Techno-Ästhetik setzt Carole Collet auf eine emotionale, fast verspielt und traditionell anmutende Gestaltung.

In place of a cold techno-aesthetic, Carole Collet aims for a design that has an emotional, almost playful, and traditional feel.

06
Sensitive Surfaces

Housewarming MyHome / J. Mayer H. Architects (GER) / 2007

traces of presence

Spuren in einem Raum zu hinterlassen, sich in eine Architektur „einzuschreiben", wenn auch nur temporär – dieses Potenzial bieten thermosensitive Oberflächen. Auf einem ähnlichen Funktionsprinzip wie Carole Collets „poetische Stoffe" beruhend, schafft der Architekt Jürgen Mayer H. mit Installationen wie **Housewarming MyHome** für das Vitra Design Museum dynamische Räume, die sich optisch verändern. Bereiche der Oberflächen von Wand- und Sitzelementen wurden mit thermosensitiver Farbe beschichtet, die bei Erwärmung verblasst. Eingelassene Wärmedrähte, die programmgesteuert zugeschaltet werden konnten, erzeugten feine helle Liniengeflechte als temporäres Ornament, das aus dem Nichts auftauchte und mit Abkühlung wieder verschwand. Zudem reagierte die Installation auf die Körperwärme anwesender Besucher. Oberflächenmuster lassen sich in solchen Räumen immer wieder neu erzeugesn – bewusst oder zufällig. Berührung wird in visuelle Spuren übersetzt – Präsenz, Aktivität, Nutzung des Raumes werden ablesbar, ihre Flüchtigkeit um einen Moment verlängert.

To leave behind traces in a space, to "write yourself into" an architecture, even if only temporarily—this is the potential of thermosensitive surfaces. In installations such as **Housewarming MyHome** for the Vitra Design Museum, architect Jürgen Mayer H. uses a similar functional principle to Carole Collet's "poetic textiles" to create dynamic spaces that change optically. Areas on the surfaces of wall and seating elements were coated with thermosensitive paint, which fades when it is heated. Hidden heating wires were controlled by a program to switch on and create a netting of fine bright lines as a temporary ornament that emerged from nowhere and then vanished again as they cooled. Beyond this, the installation reacted to the body heat of the visitors. New surface patterns can be constantly created in these spaces—consciously or accidentally. Touch is translated into visual traces—presence, activity, use of the space becomes readable, its fleetingness prolonged for a moment.

07
The Sound of Space

Otto (Madsounds) / Duncan Wilson, Manolis Kelaidis (UK) / 2006
Mix House / Karen Van Lengen, Ben Rubin, Joel Sanders (USA) / 2006

Otto (griechisch für Ohr) wurde als
Prototyp in der Ausstellung IDE Performance
Show 2006 ausgestellt.

Otto (Greek for ear) was exhibited as a
prototype in the Exhibition IDE Performance
Show 2006.

Sowohl das, was mit uns im Raum ist, als
auch das, was sich außerhalb dessen befindet, klingt, vibriert, knistert, summt, zwitschert,
plätschert, scheppert, brummt – je nachdem,
wo wir gerade sind. Viele dieser Geräusche
sind jedoch zu schwach, um für das menschliche Ohr wahrnehmbar zu sein, oder durch gut
isolierte Fenster und Fassaden abgeschirmt.

Otto und Mix House zeigen Möglichkeiten
auf, Innen- und Außenraum nicht nur visuell,
sondern auch auditiv erfahrbar zu machen.
Durch Otto werden verborgene Geräusche
hörbar. Das Gerät reagiert auf geringste Schwin-
gungen, zum Beispiel der Wand, wenn jemand
einen Raum betritt, oder das Knistern von
Eiswürfeln in einem Wasserglas, und gibt diese
verstärkt als Geräusche über einen Lautsprecher
wieder. Otto kann fast überall fixiert werden
und so durch den Einsatz mehrerer Geräte
gleichzeitig und individuelle Lautstärkeregulie-
rung einen raumspezifischen Soundtrack aus
„Madsounds" generieren. Mix House spiegelt
Geräusche der Umgebung mithilfe sogenannter
„audiovisueller" Aussichtsfenster im Inneren
des Hauses wider. Bewohner können diese in
der „Sound-Kommando-Zentrale" des Hauses
individuell abrufen und zusammenstellen.

Not only that which is in a space with us,
but also that which is outside of it sounds,
vibrates, crackles, hums, twitters, splashes,
rattles, drones—dependent on where we
currently are. But many of these noises are
too faint to be perceived by the human ear,
or they are shielded by well-isolated windows
and façades.

Otto and Mix House demonstrate ways
of making internal and external space not
only visually, but also acoustically experienceable. Otto makes hidden sounds
audible. The device reacts to the slightest
vibrations, for example in the wall, when
someone enters a room, or the crackle
of icecubes in a glass of water, and plays
them back as amplified sounds through a
speaker. Otto can be fixed in almost any
position, and through the simultaneous use
of multiple devices and individual volume
control, a space-specific soundtrack of
"Madsounds" can be generated. Mix House
mirrors the sounds of the surrounding
area using so-called "audiovisual" viewing
windows inside the house. These can be
individually retrieved and mixed together
in the house's "sound-command-centre."

Mix House wurde von den Architekten Joel Sanders und Karen Van Lengen gemeinsam mit dem Sounddesigner Ben Rubin für die Ausstellung „Open House – Intelligent Living by Design" entwickelt. Der Entwurf schlägt ein Haus mit drei speziell geschwungenen akustischen Fenstern vor, die wie audiovisuelle Teleskope funktionieren. Ein integriertes Mikrofon nimmt zielgerichtet Töne aus der Umgebung und Satellitensignale auf und überträgt diese an ein internes Audio-System, das den Klang an Lautsprecher im ganzen Haus verteilt. Zugleich zeichnet eine Kamera die Szene auf. In der „Sound-Kommando-Zentrale" in der Küche des Hauses können die synchronisierten Bilder und Klänge durch die Bewohner aktiviert und arrangiert werden.

Mix House was developed by architects Joel Sanders and Karen Van Lengen, together with the sound-designer Ben Rubin for the Exhibition "Open House—Intelligent Living by Design." The design proposes a house with specially curved acoustic windows, that function as audiovisual telescopes. An integrated microphone specifically selects sounds from the environment and satellite signals and relays these to an internal audio system, which distributes the sound around the whole house. At the same time, a camera records the scene. In the "sound-command-center" in the kitchen, the synchronized pictures and sounds can be activated and arranged by the occupants.

listen to your space

MICROPHONE/CAMERA

BELLOWS MECHANISM

08
Robots

Technological Dream Series: No. 1 Robots /
Dunne & Raby (UK) / 2007

„Aber die sehen doch gar nicht aus wie
Roboter!" – Genau diese Verwirrung wollen
Dunne & Raby provozieren. Vermutlich werden
Roboter in Zukunft eine immer wichtigere Rolle
in unserem Alltag spielen. In Japan etwa, dessen
Bevölkerung den höchsten Altersdurchschnitt
weltweit aufweist, sollen menschenähnliche
Roboter, sogenannte Humanoide, bereits in
wenigen Jahren zur Altenpflege eingesetzt
werden. Während Designer normalerweise
darum bemüht sind, Technologien benutzer-
freundlicher und attraktiver zu gestalten, wollen
uns Dunne & Raby mit ihren imaginären Pro-
dukten zu einer Debatte über die Möglichkeiten
(und Gefahren) neuer Technologien anstacheln.
Kritisch und humorvoll fokussieren sie hier auf
unser emotionales Verhältnis zu hochentwickel-
ten Technologieobjekten im eigenen Zuhause:
Ihre Roboter-Prototypen brauchen viel Zuwendung, sind neurotisch oder müssen sich
ganz genau vergewissern, mit wem sie es
gerade zu tun haben…

"But they don't look anything like robots!"—
it is just this confusion that Dunne & Raby want
to provoke. In the future Robots will presumably
play an increasingly important role in our daily
lives. In Japan, for example, where the population
has the highest average age of any other country
in the world, human-looking robots, so-called
humanoids, are intended to be deployed in a
few years' time in aged care.

While designers usually work to make technologies more user-friendly and attractive, Dunne
& Raby want their imaginary products to spark
a debate about the possibilities (and dangers)
of new technologies. Critically and humorously,
they focus on our emotional relationship to
highly-developed technology objects in our
own homes: their robot prototypes require a
great deal of attention, are neurotic, or have to
make very sure of whom they are currently
dealing with …

What kind of relationship will we establish
with robots in the future? Will they become
some kind of "technological flatmates"? How
will we communicate with them? And what
should they at all look like?

techno roommates

Was für eine Beziehung werden wir in Zukunft zu Robotern aufbauen? Werden sie
zu einer Art „technologischem Mitbewohner"?
Wie werden wir mit ihnen kommunizieren?
Und wie sollen sie überhaupt aussehen?

autistic

Robot 1 Dieser Roboter lebt in seiner eigenen Welt. Wir wissen nicht genau, was er tut, wahrscheinlich aber ist er unheimlich schlau. Er hat nur eine Eigenart: Er flüchtet vor elektromagnetischen Feldern, wie sie etwa durch Mobiltelefone oder Radios ausgelöst werden, da sie bei ihm Störungen verursachen könnten. Sobald er elektromagnetische Felder registriert, flieht er in den Bereich des Raumes mit der geringsten Strahlung. Für seinen Besitzer ist das von Vorteil: Steht er in der Mitte des Rings, befindet er sich immer an dem Ort mit der geringsten Strahlenbelastung.

Robot 2 Dieser Roboter ist ein neurotischer Sicherheitsfanatiker. Er ist so nervös, dass er jede Person, die den Raum betritt, genau analysiert mit seinen vielen Augen. Kommt ihm jemand zu nah, wird er sehr aufgeregt, sogar hysterisch. Das häusliche Sicherheitssystem könnte von dieser Roboter-Neurose profitieren.

Robot 1 This robot lives in its own world. We don't know exactly what it does; but it is probably very clever. It has one quirk: it runs away from electromagnetic fields such as those caused by mobile phones or radios, as these can cause it to malfunction. As soon as it detects an electromagnetic field, it flees to the part of the room with the least emissions. For the owner this is an advantage: if they stand in the middle of the ring, they are in the place with the least electromagnetic emissions.

Robot 2 This robot is a neurotic security fanatic. It is so nervous that it uses its many eyes to analyze precisely every person that enters the room. If someone comes too close, it becomes extremely agitated and even hysterical. The home security system could make good use of this robot's neurosis.

neurotic

55

Robot 3 Immer mehr Informationen über uns, auch unsere persönlichsten und geheimsten, werden in elektronischen Datenbanken gespeichert. Wie stellen wir sicher, dass nur wir Zugang dazu haben? Dieser Roboter fungiert als „Wachposten": Er besitzt einen eingebauten Netzhautscanner zur Personenerkennung und entscheidet so, für wen unsere Daten verfügbar sind. In Filmen genügt meist ein kurzer Blick, um die Netzhaut abzutasten. Diesem Roboter aber muss man länger in die Augen schauen. Er braucht eine Weile, um sich zu vergewissern, wer genau ihn da anschaut.

Robot 3 More and more information about us, including the most personal and private, is being stored in digital databases. How do we ensure that only we can access it? This robot functions as a "sentinel": it uses retinal scanning technology to decide who accesses our data. In films, a quick glance is usually all that is needed to scan the iris, but you have to look into the eyes of this robot for much longer. It needs time to be sure who exactly is looking at it.

Robot 4 Dieser Roboter braucht sehr viel Zuwendung. Obwohl er sehr intelligent ist, ist er in einem unterentwickelten Körper gefangen und kann sich nur mithilfe seines Besitzers fortbewegen. Der Roboter gibt ihm dadurch das Gefühl, die Kontrolle zu behalten. Ursprünglich hat er einmal unsere Sprache gesprochen, mit der Zeit jedoch seine eigene entwickelt. Man kann immer noch Fragmente vertrauter Sprache erkennen.

Robot 4 This robot needs a great deal of attention. Although extremely smart, it is trapped in an underdeveloped body and depends on its owner to move it about. The robot thus gives the owner the feeling that they are still in control. Originally it spoke our language, but over time it has evolved its own. One still recognizes in it fragments of familiar language.

needy

09
Shelter

Faraday Chair / Dunne & Raby (UK) / 1995

Durch die steigende Anzahl elektronischer Geräte sind wir einer immer stärkeren Strahlenbelastung ausgesetzt – durch robotische Hausbewohner und Möbel, interaktive Wände und ständig aktivierte Sensoren möglicherweise zukünftig noch viel mehr. Brauchen wir bald einen Zufluchtsort vor zunehmendem Elektrosmog im eigenen Zuhause? Die Installation **Faraday Chair** richtet den Blick auf unsere Verletzlichkeit und Unsicherheit gegenüber den gesundheitlichen Auswirkungen der Technologien, die wir manchmal so enthusiastisch zu begrüßen scheinen. Benannt nach Michael Faraday, einem Pionier auf dem Gebiet der Eletrotechnik, der unter anderem die elektromagnetische Induktion entdeckte, ist der Faraday Chair ein Prototyp für einen solchen Schutz-raum. Als Zufluchtsort von minimalen Dimensionen und Komfort ist er gerade groß genug, einer Person in fötaler Lage Platz zu bieten. Während die Körperhaltung an die Geborgenheit eines Babys im Mutterleib erinnert, weckt der Faraday Chair gleichzeitig beängs-tigende Assoziationen: Gefangen in einem transparenten Kasten – kaum eine Bewegung oder gar ein Aufrichten ist möglich – besteht einzig über den schnorchelartigen Schlauch eine Verbindung zur Außenwelt.

The increase in the number of electronic devices means that we are exposed to ever more electromagnetic radiation—in the future, with robotic house occupants and furniture, interactive walls, and continuously activse sensors, possibly much more. Will we soon need places of refuge from the increasing electrosmog in our own homes? The installation **Faraday Chair** turns our attention to our vulnerability and insecurity in the face of the health effects of the technologies that we sometimes seem to greet so enthusiastically. Named after Michael Faraday, a pioneer of electric technology, who discovered among other things electromagnetic induction, the Faraday Chair is a prototype for such a protective space. As a refuge of minimal dimensions and comfort, it is just large enough to take one person in fetal position. While the body position is reminiscent of the protected-ness of a baby in the womb, the Faraday chair at the same time awakens frightening associations: imprisoned in a trans-parent box—it is hardly possible to even move or sit up—the only connection to the outside world is through a snorkel-like tube.

Technopoetry

Emotional verbunden
Emotionally connected

Sie wird als „unsichtbare Architektur"[1] bezeichnet, als „aurale Architektur"[2] oder „Architektur eines räumlichen Bewusstseins"[3]. Es geht um die Sphäre, in der Raumbildung über das rein Visuelle hinausgeht und weitere menschliche Sinne wie den Hör- oder Tastsinn einbezieht – in der individuelle Erinnerungen, Emotionen und Assoziationen zur Identifizierung mit einem Raum beitragen, zur „inneren Erfahrung einer externen (räumlichen) Realität"[4].

Bietet die Verbindung von Architektur und Technologie Möglichkeiten, diese „aurale" Qualität eines Raumes zu verstärken bzw. bewusster damit umzugehen und sie in den Entwurfsprozess einzubeziehen?

„Ich werde keinen Philips-Pavillon bauen, sondern ein elektronisches Gedicht." Le Corbusier hat das „poetische" Potenzial, das in der Verbindung von Architektur und Technologie liegen kann, bereits 1959 bei seiner Rauminszenierung für die Firma Philips auf der Weltausstellung in Brüssel erkannt.[5] Mittlerweile gibt es zahlreiche Architekten und Designer, die sich vor allem mit den emotionalen Qualitäten, die neue Technologien in

It is described as "invisible architecture,"[1] as "aural architecture"[2] or "architecture of spatial consciousness"[3]. It is about the sphere in which the formation of space goes beyond the visual and includes other human senses such as hearing or touch—in which individual memories, emotions and associations contribute to identification with a space, to the "inner experience of an external (spatial) reality."[4]

Does the connection of architecture and technology offer possibilities for strengthening this "aural" quality of a space or dealing with it more consciously and integrating it into the design process?

"I will build not a Philips-Pavillion, but an electronic poem." Le Corbusier already recognized the "poetic" potential in the conjunction of architecture and technology with his 1959 spatial installation for the company Philips at the 1959 Brussels World Expo.[5] There are now many architects and designers who engage primarily with the emotional qualities of new technology in affecting our perception of space and identification with a built environment. The projects presented on

Bezug auf unsere Raumwahrnehmung, unsere Identifizierung mit einer gebauten Umgebung haben, beschäftigen. Die auf den vorherigen Seiten vorgestellten Projekte fokussieren dabei vor allem auf die Sphäre des Zuhauses und beleuchten die Frage der (emotionalen) Behausung oder Entfremdung durch Technologie.

Kann durch die Integration von Technologie in unseren Wohnraum, in Designobjekte und Alltagsgegenstände, eine emotionalere Verbindung zwischen uns und unserer direkten, aber auch weit entfernt liegenden Umgebung aufgebaut werden? Oder wollen wir in unseren vier Wänden nicht manchmal beschützt sein vor allen äußeren Einflüssen, ganz ohne Hightech und Interaktivität? Wie durchlässig ist unsere „Grenze" zur Außenwelt, wie sorgfältig trennen wir zwischen öffentlich und privat? Diese Fragen haben uns zu der vorangestellten Projektauswahl inspiriert. Die gezeigten Beispiele einer von Technologie inspirierten „Poetik des Raumes" – von Tobi Schneidlers Anwendungen für das verbundene, aber auch das „vereinsamte" Haus, von Carole Collets poetischen Stoffen über Jürgen Mayer H.s auf Berührung reagierende Rauminszenierungen bis zu den ironischen Kommentaren des britischen Designerduos Dunne & Raby – bilden dabei nur ein sehr kleines Spektrum ab. Sie präsentieren keine endgültigen, umfassenden Antworten, aber sie regen uns zur weiteren Auseinandersetzung mit dem emotionalen, vielleicht auch poetischen Potenzial von Technologie an.

Der Philosoph Otto Friedrich Bollnow hat bereits in den 1960er Jahren „Die Räumlichkeit des menschlichen Lebens"[6] beschrieben.

the preceding pages focus above all on the domain of the home, and illuminate the question of (emotionally) accommodating or alienating with technology.

Can the integration of technology into our living space, in design pieces and everyday objects, build for us an emotional connection to our immediate environment, but then also to a far distant environment? Or do we not perhaps want to be above all protected from external influences, without high-tech and interactivity, when we are within our own four walls? How permeable is our "boundary" to the external world, how carefully do we divide between public and private? These are the questions that inspired us in the preceding selection of projects. The examples here of a technology-inspired "poetry of space"—whether it be Tobi Schneidler's applications for a connected house, or on the other hand the "lonely" house, from Carole Collet's poetic fabrics to Jürgen Mayer H.'s touch-reactive installations, through to the ironic commentaries of the British designer duo Dunne & Raby—show just a small spectrum of the possibilities. They present no final, comprehensive answers, but they stimulate us to further engagement with the emotional, perhaps also poetic potential of technology.

Already in the 1960s, the philosopher Otto Friedrich Bollnow described "the spatiality of human life."[6] In every one of us, there is in the first instance a naive trust in space, a childish sense of security that can in later life continue into a natural or "unreflecting security in house and home." This security is often threatened

Jedem Menschen wohne zunächst ein naives Vertrauen zum Raum inne, ein kindliches Geborgensein, das sich dann im späteren Leben als natürliches oder „gedankenloses Geborgensein in Haus und Heimat" fortsetzen kann. Oftmals werde diese Geborgenheit aber von einem Zustand der Heimatlosigkeit oder Unbehaustheit abgelöst. Der Raum offenbart sich in seiner Unheimlichkeit und Fremdheit. Daraus ergibt sich, so Bollnow, die erste „Forderung für das wahre Wohnen" – sich einen „Eigenraum der Geborgenheit zu schaffen". Allerdings drohe dabei die Gefahr, sich im Innenraum abzukapseln. Deshalb müsse man auch den bedrohlichen und gefährlichen Außenraum voll in das Leben einbeziehen, um „die ganze Spannung zwischen den Räumen auszuhalten, in der sich allein menschliches Leben füllen kann. (…) So besteht die dritte Forderung darin, sich im Hause wohnend zugleich jenem größeren Ganzen des Raumes anvertrauen zu können."[7] Projekte wie Otto (S. 48) oder Mix House (S. 50) die den Außenraum und bisher verborgene Klangwelten des Innenraums in unser Zuhause holen, bieten hier möglicherweise Ansätze, Außen und Innen zum „größeren Ganzen des Raumes" auf poetische Art und Weise zu verbinden. Eine andere Antwort liefert das Projekt Remote Home:

Remote Home fokussierte auf physische und emotionale Interaktionen anstatt auf visuelle Schnittstellen und Verbindungen. Es ging darum, etwas Poetisches zu erschaffen, wo „Zuhause" lebendig und durch die Aktivitäten und Rituale seiner Bewohner zum Leben erweckt wird. Der häusliche Bereich wird zu einer Erweiterung des Körpers. Beide Woh-

however by a state of homelessness or a lack of comodation. Space reveals itself in its uncanniness and foreignness. From this emerges, according to Bollnow, the original "demand for a true dwelling"—to "build one's own space of security." The danger here, however, is that of shutting oneself off in this interior space. One would thus have to also fully integrate the threatening and dangerous exterior space into one's life, in order to "withstand the full tension between the spaces, in which alone a human life can be filled out. ... The third demand is thus that in living in our home we must at the same time trust in this larger totality of space."[7] Projects such as Otto (p. 48) or Mix House (p. 50), which bring outside space or formerly hidden sound-worlds of our inner space into our homes, offer perhaps approaches for connecting outer and inner into a "greater totality of space" in a poetic way. Another answer is offered by the project Remote Home:

Remote Home focused on physical and emotional interactions as opposed to visual interfaces and connections. It aimed at creating a sense of poetics; where "home" is alive and comes to life only through the actions and rituals of its inhabitants. The domestic space becomes an extension of the body. Both flats were fitted with sensory and kinetic devices which enabled their inhabitants to share a sense of being together, connected beyond geographical boundaries.[8]

This is how the British textile designer Carole Collet describes the essence of the project for which she designed the kinetic wall. For Tobi Schneidler, the initiator of Remote

nungen waren mit Sensoren und kinetischen Geräten ausgestattet, die es ihren Bewohnern ermöglichten, sich beieinander zu fühlen, verbunden über geografische Grenzen hinweg.[8]

So beschreibt die britische Textildesignerin Carole Collet die Essenz des Projektes, für das sie das Design der kinetischen Wand entworfen hat. Für den Initiator von Remote Home, Tobi Schneidler, war das Projekt auch durch sehr persönliche Erfahrungen motiviert, wie er im Gespräch mit plan a berichtete:

Ich hatte eine Fernbeziehung in Paris und war selber beruflich in Stockholm und in London tätig und habe überlegt, was bedeutet es überhaupt, ein Zuhause zu haben, wie sieht eine Wohnung aus für mich, wo ich doch so fragmentiert lebe und viel unterwegs bin. Aus diesem Überlegen heraus entstand der Ansatz, das Konzept von Telepräsenz in Wohnungen zu integrieren.

Telepräsenz ist ein Thema, das zum damaligen Zeitpunkt vor allem im Büro- und Arbeitskontext zum Beispiel in Form von Videokonferenzen Anwendung fand. Ich wollte aber eine eher emotionale Dimension schaffen und untersuchen, wie man die Telepräsenz emotional und taktil auch in das Design einer Wohnung integrieren kann, in Möbelstücken, in elektronischen Gegenständen usw. und wie dadurch eine Wohnung nicht nur an einem Ort sein, sondern sich an zwei Orten gleichzeitig befinden kann. Eine Fernbeziehung hat etwas mit Liebe zu tun und da spielt es keine Rolle, perfekt via PowerPoint zu kommunizieren, sondern es geht eher darum, kleine Alltags-

Home, the project was also motivated by very personal experiences, as he explained in conversation with plan a:

I had a long-distance relationship in Paris and was myself working professionally in Stockholm and London, and I was thinking about what it means to have a place that is home, what an apartment should look like for me, given that I live in such a fragmented way and am constantly on the move. These thoughts were the starting point for the idea of integrating the concept of telepresence into apartments.

Telepresence is an approach that was being used at that time above all in an office and work context, for example in the form of video conferences. But I wanted to create an emotional dimension and explore how telepresence can be integrated into an apartment in an emotional and tactile way, in furniture, electric devices etc., and how an apartment can thereby be not just in one place, but in two places at once. A long distance relationship is about love, and here it is not a matter of communicating perfectly by PowerPoint, but rather about sharing the little everyday moments. Tiny things, that show the presence of a partner, without having to be "high-definition," without the other actually having to sit across from you, but rather giving a feeling of being together, sharing something.

At that time, the beginning of the 2000s, Electrolux, Sony Ericsson, Samsung, and the others all presented their Smart Homes and Smart Kitchens. In all of these projects the

momente teilen zu können. Kleine Elemente, die die Präsenz des Partners zeigen, ohne „hochauflösend" zu sein, ohne dass der andere jetzt wirklich gegenüber sitzt, sondern eher das Gefühl des Zusammenseins, des Teilens. Zu dieser Zeit, Anfang der 2000er, haben Elektrolux, Sony Ericsson, Samsung alle ihre Smart Homes und Smart Kitchens vorgestellt. In all diesen Projekten war der Ansatz immer funktional. Da ging es vor allem darum, durch Technologie klare Funktionen zu erfüllen, wie zum Beispiel Klimasteuerung, Sicherheit, Lichtsteuerung. Mir ging es bei Remote Home um etwas anderes. Wie kann Technologie auch etwas „Nettes" sein? Etwas, das man sich nicht nur um der Funktion willen anschafft, sondern weil es auch Spaß macht oder weil es eben ermöglicht, emotional über Distanz zu kommunizieren und in eine andere Beziehung mit seinen häuslichen Objekten zu treten.[9]

Letzterer Aspekt wird in Projekten wie Robotic Furniture von Tobi Schneidler (S. 42) oder in den Hausrobotern von Dunne & Raby (S.52) deutlich. Gegenstände in unserem Zuhause werden zu „sozial intelligenten" Objekten, über die wir nicht mehr mit anderen in Verbindung treten, sondern die direkt mit uns kommunizieren. Die Fernbeziehung existiert nicht mehr? Dann wird die Verbindung gekappt, die Bank, die uns bisher die Präsenz des Liebsten anzeigt, umfunktioniert zum eigenwilligen Mitbewohner, der immer wieder unerwartet durch Bewegungen auf sich aufmerksam macht. Nebenbei kümmern wir uns um den nach Aufmerksamkeit bettelnden Roboter von Dunne & Raby … Ihre Technological Dream Series von Dunne & Raby mag

approach was uniform and always functional. The aim was primarily to use technology to fulfill clear functions, such as for example climate control, security, lighting control. I had a different aim with Remote Home. How can technology be something "nice"? Something that one acquires not just to fulfill some function, but because it is fun or because it makes it possible to communicate emotionally across distances and to take up a different relationship to domestic objects.[9]

This last aspect is articulated in projects like Robotic Furniture by Tobi Schneidler (p. 42) or in the house-robots of Dunne & Raby (p. 52). Objects in our home become "socially intelligent" objects, which no longer connect us to others, but rather communicate with us directly. The long-distance relationship no longer exists? Then the line of communication is shut off, and the bench, which formerly signaled the presence of the loved one, changes its function into a self-willed flatmate, continually making its presence known through unexpected movements. Meanwhile we are busy looking after the attention-seeking robots of Dunne & Raby… The Technological Dream Series could be understood above all as an ironic investigation of the influence of technology on our daily lives. In various interviews, Dunne & Raby described their working approach:

It is still about form and function. Just that the form might no longer be physical or tangible, and function might not be so pragmatic but instead more metaphysical. Design can only follow our needs and desires, it can't create them. If your desires remain unimaginative and

vor allem als ironische Auseinandersetzung mit dem Einfluss von Technologie auf unser Alltagsleben verstanden werden können. In verschiedenen Interviews haben Dunne & Raby ihren Arbeitsansatz so beschrieben:

Es geht uns schon noch um Form und Funktion. Nur dass die Form möglicherweise nicht mehr physisch oder tangibel oder die Funktion nicht mehr so pragmatisch, sondern eher metaphysischer sein könnte. Design kann nur unseren Bedürfnissen und Wünschen folgen, es kann sie nicht schaffen. Wenn die Bedürfnisse fantasielos und praktisch bleiben, dann wird Design so sein. Ich glaube, in unseren Projekten hoffen wir auf eine Zeit, zu der wir komplexere und subtilere Alltagsbedürfnisse haben werden als heute. Unsere Objekte sind in Antizipation dieser Zeit entworfen. Geduldig wartend. Vielleicht sind sie utopisch.[10]

Die Welt, in der wir heute leben, ist unglaublich komplex, unsere sozialen Beziehungen, Wünsche, Fantasien, Hoffnungen und Ängste unterscheiden sich sehr von denen zu Beginn des 20. Jahrhunderts. Die Rolle, die Techno-logie in unserer Alltagserfahrung heute spielt, ist beispiellos. (…) Statt den Einzug von Technologie in unser Alltagsleben zu beschleunigen, sollten wir über ihre Auswirkungen nachdenken und uns sogar fragen, ob wir das tatsächlich brauchen.[11]

Die Designerin Carole Collet sieht im Einsatz von Technologie vor allem Potenzial für die Schaffung emotionalerer, poetischerer Momente. In einem Interview mit plan a beschrieb sie ihr

practical, then that is what design will be. I guess in our projects, we are hoping for a time when we will have more complex and subtle everyday needs than we do today. Our objects are designed in anticipation of that time. Patiently waiting. Maybe they are utopian.[10]…

The world we live in today is incredibly complex, our social relations, desires, fantasies, hopes and fears are very different from those at the beginning of the 20th century. The role technology plays today in shaping our experience of everyday life is unprecedented. … Rather than speeding up the entry of technology into everyday life, we need to reflect on its impact and ask if we even need it.[11]

Primarily, the designer Carole Collet sees in the application of technology the potential for the creation of more emotional, poetic moments. In an interview with plan a, she described the research interest that determines her work in the context of "Poetic Textiles for Smart Homes" (p. 44) in the following way:

For me, a poetic textile plays with mixed references, anachronisms, metaphors as well as narratives. As opposed to being purely functional or decorative and "fixed" in time, a poetic textile brings another dimension into place, be it by playing with unexpected materials or by creating a another level of interaction that teases out our domestic rituals.

I am fascinated by our collective perception of future homes. In the 60s, 70, 80s and 90s, our home of the futures were often portrayed as technology-driven spaces. MIT, Philips,

Forschungsinteresse, das ihre Arbeiten im Rahmen von „Poetic Textiles for Smart Homes" (S. 44) maßgeblich bestimmt, folgendermaßen:

Poetische Textilien spielen mit verschiedensten Referenzen, Anachronismen, Metaphern ebenso wie mit Erzählungen. Anstatt rein funktional oder dekorativ und in der Zeit „fixiert" zu sein, bringen poetische Textilien eine andere Dimension ein, sei es, indem sie mit unerwarteten Materialien spielen oder dadurch, dass eine andere Ebene der Interaktion geschaffen wird, die unsere häuslichen Rituale „herauskitzelt".

Ich bin von der kollektiven Wahrnehmung von Zukunftshäusern fasziniert. In den 60ern, 70ern, 80ern und 90ern wurden unsere Häuser der Zukunft oftmals als durch Technologie dominierte Räume dargestellt. MIT, Philips, Orange haben etwa Prototypen entwickelt, die durch „hard intelligent ware" bestimmt waren, und ich glaube, dass Textilien diese Wahrnehmung der Zukunft herausfordern können, indem sie den Bereich der Erfahrungen und Rituale in das Konzept von Zuhause einbringen. Wie können Textilien intelligente Technologien und Materialien wieder mit der Idee von Geschichte, Handwerk und Ökologie verbinden und damit die Rolle von Textilien im übermächtigen architektonischen Kontext neu definieren? „Poetic Textiles for Smart Homes" ist eine Designuntersuchung, in deren Rahmen innovative Textilien für den häuslichen Markt entwickelt werden sollen. Indem ästhetische, funktionale und ethische Fragestellungen untersucht werden, will das Projekt neue Möglichkeiten für Textilien aufzeigen, um eine

Orange for instance have developed prototypes driven by hard intelligent ware, and I believe that textiles can challenge that perception of the future by bringing the notion of domestic into the realms of rituals and experience. How can textiles reconnect the notion of history, craft, and ecology with intelligent technologies and materials, thus redefining the role of textiles within an overpowering architectural context? "Poetic Textiles For Smart Homes" is a design quest which aims at developing innovative textiles for the domestic market. By investigating issues of aesthetics, functions, and ethics, the project aims at mapping out new possibilities for textiles to take a leading role in redefining our intimate and emotional relationship with "smart homes."[12]

Carole Collet takes this conception a step further with her current work on "Poetic Textiles for Smart Homes". Since the so-called smart fabrics require, in her opinion, too much energy for operation and are difficult to recycle, she is increasingly concentrating on "natural technologies" and is investigating, for example, the potential of organic photosynthesis for the development of textile surfaces and furniture pieces that change their form under UV-light.

1 Vgl. z.B. Anna Barbara / Anthony Perliss: Invisible Architecture, Skira 2006 (Untersuchung zur Erfahrung von Räumen und Architektur durch den Geruchssinn), aber auch die Arbeiten des französischen Architekten Philippe Rahm, der unter dem Titel „Invisible Architectures" verschiedene Faktoren für die Bildung von Raumatmosphären (z.B. Temperatur) untersucht / See, e.g., Anna Barbara / Anthony Perliss: Invisible Architecture, Skira 2006 (Investigation on the experience of spaces and architecture with the sense of

führende Rolle in der Neudefinition unserer persönlichen und emotionalen Beziehung zu „Smart Homes" einzunehmen.[12]

Dabei geht Carole Collet mit ihren aktuellen Arbeiten im Rahmen von „Poetic Textiles for Smart Homes" sogar noch einen Schritt weiter. Weil die sogenannten „smarten" Textilien ihrer Ansicht nach zu viel Energie für den Betrieb benötigen und sich schwierig recyceln lassen, konzentriert sie sich verstärkt auf „natürliche Technologien" und untersucht zum Beispiel das Potenzial organischer Fotosynthese für die Entwicklung von textilen Oberflächen und Möbelstücken, die unter UV-Licht ihre Form verändern.

smell), but also the work of the French architect Philippe Rahm, who has investigated various factors (e.g. temperature) in the establishment of spatial atmospheres in "Invisible Architectures."

2 Vgl. z.B. / See e.g., Barry Blesser / Linda-Ruth Salter: Spaces Speak – Are You Listening?, MIT Press 2007

3 Vgl. z.B. / See e.g. Joy Monice Malnar / Frank Vodvarka: Sensory Design, University of Minnesota Press 2004

4 Blesser / Salter 2007, S. / p. 131

5 Der Philips Pavillon gilt als erste elektronisch gesteuerte Architektur und als Prototyp eines dynamischen Raumes. / The Philips Pavilion is considered the first electronically controlled architecture and prototype of a dynamic space. Vgl. / See Philipp Oswalt: „Techno-Fiction. Zur Kritik der technologischen Utopien", in: Thesis. Wissenschaftliche Zeitschrift der Bauhaus-Universität Weimar, Bd. / Vol. 2, Heft / Journal 3/4, 1997, S. / p. 275 ff.

6 Vgl. / see Otto Friedrich Bollnow: Mensch und Raum, Kohlhammer 1963 / Textquelle für die folgenden Zitate / Text source for the following citations: Otto Friedrich Bollnow: „Die Räumlichkeit des menschlichen Lebens" in: Àkos Moravánsky / Katalin M. Gyöngy: Architekturtheorie im 20. Jahrhundert. Eine kritische Anthologie, Springer 2003, S. / p. 236 ff.

7 ebd., S. / ibid., p. 238

8 Carole Collet: „A Poetic Cyber-Quest", Konferenzbeitrag, veröffentlicht in / conference contribution, published in: Space Between, The Conference Proceedings Volume 2, Curtin University of Technology 2006

9 Interview Tobi Schneidler mit / with plan a, 09.02.2009

10 Interview mit / with Anthony Dunne, in: Christoph Brändle: Wouldn't It Be Nice… Wishful Thinking in Art and Design, JRP Ringier 2008, Textquelle: Onlineveröffentlichung / text source: online publication: http://dunneandraby.co.uk/content/bydandr/97/0

11 Fictional Functions and Functional Fictions, Interview mit / with Dunne & Raby, in: Troika: Digital by Design. Crafting Technology for Products and Environments, Thames + Hudson 2008, Textquelle: Onlineveröffentlichung / text source: online publication: http://dunneandraby.co.uk/content/bydandr/46/0

12 Schriftliches Interview / written interview Carole Collet mit / with plan a, 26.01.2009

II.
PUBLIC
(ATMO)SPHERE

Kommunikation und Kontrolle im öffentlichen Raum
Communication and Control in Public Space

Durch die Integration von Technologie an Gebäuden, durch Medienfassaden, Licht- und Videoinstallationen, wird der öffentliche Raum zum „Sensing Space" – zum wahrnehmenden Raum, der kommuniziert und zunehmend die Grenze zwischen Innen und Außen, zwischen privatem und öffentlichem Raum, zwischen Individuum und anonymer Masse aufhebt. Welche neuen Formen der Kommunikation werden durch die Verbindung von Architektur und Technologie ermöglicht? Wie kann der Einzelne im öffentlichen Raum Spuren hinterlassen, sich mit seiner Umgebung verbunden fühlen?

Dabei stellt sich im öffentlichen Raum noch stärker die Frage von Selbstbestimmung und Fremdkontrolle: sensitiv überreizt – vielleicht auch schon entsprechend manipuliert – durch dauersendende Werbefassaden, wanken wir, dank GPS-Navigation dennoch zielstrebig, durch die Stadt ins nächste Einkaufszentrum, jede unserer Bewegungen von Überwachungskameras verfolgt … Die im Kapitel PUBLIC (ATMO)SPHERE vorgestellten Projekte zeigen, dass die Verbindung von Technologie und Architektur weit über die Funktionalisierung von Fassaden als Werbeflächen hinaus gehen kann. Es geht hier um eine Erweiterung von Architektur, um die konzeptionelle Integration von Technologie, um die Schaffung emotionaler Momente, die uns im Alltagstrott innehalten lassen – wenn zum Beispiel Windböen plötzlich als Lichtarchitektur sichtbar werden, wenn uns das Gebäude nebenan etwas über die Stimmung unserer Nachbarn erzählt, wenn Häuserfassaden zu virtuellen Bibliotheken werden. Die Gefahr der öffentlichen Überwachung wird dabei in diesem Kapitel ebenso thematisiert wieder die der medialen Überreizung.

Through the integration of technology and buildings, through media façades, light, and video installations, public space becomes "sensing space," which communicates, and increasingly breaks down the boundary between inner and outer, between private and public space, between individual and anonymous crowd. What new forms of communication are made possible by the conjunction of architecture and technology? How can the individual leave behind traces in public space, feel connected with their surroundings?

We are confronted more than ever with the question of self-determination and external control: sensorily overloaded—and perhaps already accordingly manipulated—by continuously running advertising media façades, we stagger along, determinedly on target nevertheless thanks to our GPS-navigation, through the streets of the city and into the next shopping center, every movement followed by surveillance cameras … The projects presented in the chapter PUBLIC (ATMO)SPHERE show that the connection between technology and architecture can go far beyond the use of façades as advertising space. What we see here is the extension of architecture, the conceptual integration of technology, the creation of emotional moments that give us pause in the midst of our everyday lives—as for example when gusts of wind suddenly become visible as light architecture, or when the building next door tells us something about the mood of our neighbors, or when house façades become virtual libraries. This chapter thematizes at the same time the dangers of public surveillance and of media overload.

10
Tower of Winds

Tower of Winds / Toyo Ito & Associates (JP) / 1986

„Urban Robot", urbaner Roboter, nannte sich der japanische Meisterarchitekt Toyo Ito zu Beginn seiner Karriere. Ein Name, der seinen poetischen Arbeiten, die Architektur und Technologie auf äußerst sensible Art und Weise miteinander verbinden, fast konträr gegenübersteht und vielleicht auch deshalb von Toyo Ito seit 1979 nicht mehr verwendet wird. Sein „Turm der Winde" gilt als Pionierleistung und war lange ein Wahrzeichen von Yokohama. **Tower of Winds** entstand 1986 in der Nähe des städtischen Bahnhofs. Toyo Ito verkleidete einen bereits existierenden Turm mit verspiegelten Paneelen und einem ovalen Aluminiumzylinder. Zwischen diese beiden Schichten positionierte der Architekt ein komplexes Lichtsystem, besteht aus 1280 LED-Lampen, zwölf strahlend weißen, vertikal angebrachten Ringen aus Neonleuchten und 30 computergesteuerten Flutlichtern. Umwelteinflüsse wie Geräusche, Windstärke und -richtung veränderten die Intensität der Flutlichter und damit die Inszenierung des Turms. Dank der integrierten Technologien wird Architektur hier zum dynamischen, sich im Wechselspiel mit seiner Umwelt transformierenden Medium.

"Urban Robot" was what the Japanese master architect Toyo Ito called himself at the beginning of his career. The name seems almost to stand in contradiction to his poetic works, which bind together architecture and technology in the most sensitive way, and perhaps this is why he has not used the name since 1979. His "Tower of Winds" is considered a pioneering achievement and has been for a long time a symbol for Yokohama. **Tower of Winds** was built in 1986 near the city train station. Toyo Ito disguised an already existing tower with reflective panels and an oval aluminum cylinder. Between these two layers the architect positioned a complex light system, consisting of 1280 LED-lights, twelve beaming, white, vertically arrayed rings of neon light, and 30 computer-controlled floodlights. Environmental influences such as sounds, or force and direction of the wind, change the intensity of the floodlights and thereby the staging of the tower. Thanks to integrated technologies, architecture becomes a dynamic medium, transforming itself in an interplay with its environment.

11
Architectural Tuning

A.Amp / realities:united (GER) / 2008
UEC ILUMA / realities:united (GER) / 2009

Medienfassaden – Spielzeug der Werbewirtschaft und ein weiteres Mittel zur Steigerung
unserer visuellen Überreiztheit oder ein neues
Kommunikationspotenzial für die Architektur?
Die Fassadeninstallation **A.Amp** von realities:
united wurde entwickelt für ein Bürogebäude
von WOHA Architects in Singapur. Der Name
steht für „Architectural Advertising Amplifier".
Umschreiben lässt sich A.Amp als eine Art
„Vermittler" zwischen einem hochauflösenden
Werbebildschirm – an der Gebäudefassade
bereits vorgesehen, bevor realities:united
in das Projekt involviert wurden – und der

Media façades—a toy for the advertising
industry and another means for increasing
our visual overload, or a new communication potential for architecture? The façade
installation **A.Amp** by realities:united was
developed for an office building by WOHA
Architects in Singapore. The name stands
for "Architectural Advertising Amplifier."
A.Amp could be described as a kind of
mediator between a high-resolution advertising screen—already planned for the
building façade, before realities:united
became involved in the project—and the

Architektur selbst. Tagsüber sieht man der Fassade ihr Potenzial kaum an. Erst nachts, wenn die Räume menschenleer sind, werden die Bürofenster Teil der medialen Bespielung. Hinter der Glasfassade befinden sich über 500 LED-Bauteile, die den High-End-Monitor einfassen. Sie bilden ein niedrig auflösendes, das Gebäude großflächig umschließendes Display. Mittels einer speziellen Software werden die Animationen auf dem Werbebildschirm analysiert und auf A.Amp als visuelles Farbecho wiedergegeben. Die Installation schafft so den Sprung vom isolierten High-End-Display, typisch für so viele Werbetafeln, zu einer integrierten, im Maßstab der Architektur konzipierten Lösung.

architecture itself. During the day one hardly sees the potential of the façade. Only at night, when the rooms become deserted, do the office windows become part of a media installation. Behind the glass façade are more than 500 LED components, surrounding the high-end monitor. They form a low-definition display, enclosing large areas of the building. By way of special software, the animations on the advertising screen are analyzed, and then rendered on A.Amp as a visual color-echo. The installation thus achieves the leap from isolated high-end display, typical of so many advertising panels, to an integrated solution conceived on the level of architecture.

Die Fassade wird zu einer mehrschichtigen Collage digitaler und materieller Elemente. Büros, in denen bis spät in die Nacht gearbeitet wird, „stören" immer wieder das dynamische, durch A.Amp generierte Bild mit ihren statisch erleuchteten Fenstern.

The façade becomes a multilayered collage of digital and material elements. offices that are working long into the night "disturb" the dynamic picture generated by A.Amp with their statically lit windows.

Ursprünglich wollte der Bauherr eine „klassische" Medienfassade: „viele bunte Lampen hinter einer geschlossenen Glasfläche". realities:united haben statt dessen eine Installation entwickelt, die sich aus zahlreichen einzelnen Elementen – ähnlich kleinen Kristallen – zusammensetzt und die Grenze zwischen Display und ornamentalem Fassadengitter aufzuheben scheint. In drei verschiedenen Größen wurden die Kristalle angefertigt. Jeweils ein, drei oder sieben LEDs sind integriert. Die einzelnen Leuchtelemente sind mit einer opaken, in der Dichte variierenden Schicht bedruckt. Da sie auch das Sonnenlicht reflektieren können, funktioniert **UEC ILUMA** bei Tag und bei Nacht. Entwickelt wurde die Installation für das ILUMA Gebäude, Teil des neuen, von WOHA Architects entworfenen Urban Entertainment Center mit Theatern, Clubs, Bars und Geschäften im Singapurer Ausgehviertel Bugis.

Originally the client wanted a "classic" media façade: "lots of bright lights behind a closed glass surface." realities:united have instead developed an installation composed of many individual elements—similar to small crystals—that seems to break down the boundary between display and ornamental façade trellis. The crystals were manufactured in three different sizes and one, three, or seven LEDs are intergrated into each one. The individual light elements are covered with an opaque film of varying thickness. Since they can also reflect sunlight, **UEC ILUMA** functions both day and night. The installation was developed for the ILUMA building, part of a new Urban Entertainment Center with theaters, clubs, bars, and shops, designed by WOHA Architects for the Singapore nightlife district of Bugis.

12
Campus City

Harlem Mediatech / G TECTS (USA) / Entwurf / Design 2004
Baruch College / G TECTS (USA) / Entwurf / Design 2004

ACCESBILITY

Bibliotheken zu errichten und zu bestücken ist teuer. Das Architekturbüro G TECTS schlägt daher für den New Yorker Stadtteil Harlem ein virtuelles Bibliotheksnetzwerk vor, das in der Stadt durch interaktive Medienfassaden repräsentiert wird. Diese sollen in Baulücken und auf urbanen Brachen errichtet werden und aus mehreren Etagen bestehen, die von der Rückseite über eine Treppe und einen Fahrstuhl betreten werden können. Hinter den Fassaden der **Harlem Mediatech** sollen öffentliche Parks mit Internetzugang entstehen. Die Medienfassaden bestehen aus transparenten Touch Screens – so können Passanten auf der Vorderseite sehen, was die Nutzer auf der anderen Seite gerade lesen. Harlem wird zum Campus, die offenen (virtuellen) Zugangsmöglichkeiten zu Information und Bildung werden durch die Medienfassaden im Stadtraum sichtbar. Welche Informationen die Harlem Mediatech Filialen abbilden, wird durch die Benutzer bestimmt. Das Konzept erinnert an die Arbeiten von Cedric Price (siehe S. 114) und überträgt seinen Ansatz über die Zugänglichkeit von Bildung und Information in das digitale Zeitalter.

To build and equip libraries is costly. The architecture office G TECTS thus proposes a virtual library network for the New York Harlem district, represented in the city by interactive media façades. These would be installed in building gaps and on unused urban land, and would consist of multiple floors that can be reached from behind by stairs and an elevator. Behind the façades of the **Harlem Mediatech** there would be public parks with internet access. The media façades should consist of transparent touch-screens, and passers-´by would be able to see on the front, what the users on the other side are currently reading. Harlem would become a campus, and the open (virtual) access possibilities to information and education would become visible in the city space through the media façades. What information the Harlem Mediatech branches show on the outside would be determined by the users. The idea is reminiscent of the work of Cedric Price (see p.114), taking his approach to the accessibility of education and information into the digital age.

Auch der Entwurf von G TECTS für das **Baruch College** nutzt Technologie zur Visualisierung von Bildungsressourcen und macht diese für die Öffentlichkeit frei zugänglich. Die Sanierung und Erweiterung des Colleges in Manhattan konzentriert sich vor allem auf das Lawrence and Eris Field Building an der Lexington Avenue. Eine Medienfassade unterstreicht hier die Idee „freier Bildung": Was im Inneren des Gebäudes in den Unterrichtsräumen geschieht, wird von außen durch einen großen Bildschirm und den Einsatz von Informationstechnologie sichtbar. Passanten können so Teile des Unterrichts vom Straßenraum aus verfolgen.

The G TECTS design for **Baruch College** also uses technology to visualize educational resources and make them freely available to the public. The renovation and extension of the college in Manhattan is primarily concentrated on the Lawrence and Eris Field Building on Lexington Avenue. A media façade underlines here the idea of "free education:" what is happening inside the building in the classrooms becomes visible from the outside by way of a giant screen and the use of information technology. Passers-by can thus follow parts of the teaching from the street space.

13
Universal View

Aleph / Adam Somlai-Fischer (HU) & Bengt Sjölén (SE) / 2007

Die Medienfassade spiegelt ihre Umwelt und setzt sie in den Augen der Betrachter neu zusammen: **Aleph** besteht aus 200 computergesteuerten, beweglichen Autospiegeln. Sie reflektieren Fragmente aus der Umgebung, richten sich zum Beispiel nach bestimmten Farben wie dem Blau des Himmels, und je nach Standort des Betrachters entstehen so immer wieder neue Bilder. Über eine Kamera werden die Computer mit Informationen aus dem Umfeld – zum Beispiel mit den Positionen von Passanten, den Bewegungen der Wolken – „gefüttert" und entsprechend die Spiegel über Mikrosteuerungssysteme ausgerichtet. Was die Betrachter sehen, wird aus Fragmenten ihrer Umgebung generiert, aber es ist ein Bild, das nur für sie in der Reflexion der Spiegel existiert. Der Name Aleph erinnert an Jorge Luis Borges' gleichnamige Erzählung, in der das Aleph einen Punkt im Raum bezeichnet, von dem aus jeder, der hinein sieht, das gesamte Universum betrachten kann.

The media façade mirrors its environment and reassembles it in the eyes of the observer: **Aleph** consists of 200 computer-controlled, mobile car mirrors. They reflect fragments of the surroundings, directing themselves for example at particular colors like the blue of the sky, creating ever new images, dependent on the position of the observer. A camera "feeds" the computers with information from the environment—for example the position of passers-by, the movements of clouds—and micro-control systems then align the mirrors accordingly. What the observers see is generated from fragments of their surroundings, but it is a picture that exists for them alone, in the reflections of the mirrors. The name Aleph refers to Jorge Luis Borges' story of that name, in which the Aleph denotes a point in space, from where anyone who looks in can observe the entire universe.

Communicating Space

Architektur als Mitteilungsgenerator
Architecture as Communication Generator

[A]us Fassaden [werden] frei bespielbare Medienwände. Ihre ehemalige Bildlichkeit wird von den Medien verschlungen und bekommt damit die Bedeutung von Monitoren im XXL-Format. Diese nächtliche Verselbständigung der medialen Funktion von der Aufgabe, die das Haus samt Fassade als Teil des städtebaulichen Raumes hatte, überschreitet damit eine bisher noch gar nicht vorstellbare Grenze. Sie stellt nämlich die Rolle der Architektur als materielle Struktur der Stadt und damit den Charakter des öffentlichen Raumes in Frage.
Hans Stimmann, Senatsbaudirektor Berlin a.D.[1]

Die Fassade als ein riesiger Bildschirm, auf dem mehr oder weniger abstrakte, ständig wechselnde Bilder flimmern und ohnehin schon gestresste Großstädter noch weiter überreizen? Wie können Medienfassaden mehr sein als ein Megadisplay, das willkürlich vor ein Haus geklebt wird? Was für Mitteilungen – jenseits von Werbung – könnte ein Gebäude überhaupt in den Stadtraum senden? Wie verändert sich dadurch unsere Wahrnehmung der Stadt? Die auf den vorangegangenen Seiten vorgestellten

Façades become free for use as media walls. Their former visual prominence is engulfed by media, and they come to function as monitors in XXL-format. This nighttime activity, in which the media function becomes independent of the role that the building and its façade played as part of an urban space, oversteps a formerly unimaginable boundary. It calls into question the role of architecture as the material structure of the city, and thus also calls into question the character of public space.
Hans Stimmann, former building director Berlin[1]

The façade as an enormous screen, on which more or less abstract, continually changing images flicker, further overstimulating the already stressed city dwellers? How can media façades be more than just a megadisplay, arbitrarily stuck on the front of a house? What kinds of communication—beyond advertising—can a building at all project into the city space? How does this change our perception of the city? The projects on the preceding pages show a small cross-section

Projekte zeigen einen kleinen Ausschnitt der Möglichkeiten, die sich der Architektur durch mediale Oberflächen eröffnen. Der Tower of Winds von Toyo Ito, eine der ersten Medienfassaden überhaupt, wurde durch die poetische Verbindung von Physischem und Ephemerem zu einem Wahrzeichen von Yokohama. Der Turm eingehüllt in ein durchscheinendes, sich ständig veränderndes Kleid – die Symbiose von Architektur und Technologie als eine Art „Media-Clothing" – diesen Ansatz hat Ito immer weiter erforscht und später auch auf ganze Gebäudekonzepte übertragen, wie zum Beispiel bei seiner berühmten Sendai Mediatheque in Tokyo. Bei realities:united sind es hingegen nicht ephemere Umwelteinflüsse, die die Mitteilungen auf ihren Fassadeninstallationen generieren. Vielmehr erforschen sie in ihren Projekten gezielt eine „Ästhetik des Verhaltens" medialer Oberflächen, indem sie mit grundlegenden (architektonischen) Parametern wie Maßstab, Bildauflösung oder räumlicher Tiefe experimentieren. Sie bezeichnen ihre Arbeit selbst als „Architecture Tuning" – ihre Fassadeninstallationen wirken als Katalysatoren, die die Ausdrucksfähigkeit eines Gebäudes erweitern. Häufig werden die Pro-jekte im Anschluss kuratorisch betreut und von Künstlern bespielt.

Im Vergleich dazu sind die Projekte von G TECTS weniger an eine strenge Ästhetik geknüpft. Im Mittelpunkt steht hier ein stärker politisch orientierter Ansatz – der permanente, einfache und für jedermann verfügbare Zugang zu Wissen. Ein wesentliches Element ihrer Arbeiten ist dabei die Verknüpfung von realem und virtuellem Raum: In ihre Gebäude inte-

of the possibilities opened up to architecture through media surfaces. Toyo Ito's Tower of Winds, one of the first ever media façades, poetically combined the physical with the ephemeral, and thereby became a symbol for Yokohama. The tower wrapped in a translucent, ever changing garment—the symbiosis of architecture and technology as a kind of "media-clothing"—Ito has further explored this approach and later applied it to entire building complexes, for example, is his famous Sendai Mediatheque in Tokyo. With realities: united on the other hand, it is not ephemeral environmental influences that generate the communicated content of their façade installations. Rather, their projects specifically explore an "aesthetic of behavior" of media surfaces, by experimenting with fundamental (architectural) parameters such as scale, image resolution or spatial depth. They themselves describe their work as "architecture tuning"— their façade installations function as catalysts for expanding the expressive capabilities of a building. The projects often come under the supervision of curators and become displays for the work of artists.

In comparison, the projects of G TECTS are less tied to a strict aesthetic. What is central here is a more politically oriented interest—in lasting, simple, and universally available access to knowledge. Hence, an essential element of their works is the bringing together of real and virtual space: G TECTS integrate electronic displays into their buildings, functioning as interfaces and "windows" to further, unlimited virtual networks. The entire building, with all its internal and external spaces, becomes a

grieren G TECTS elektronische Displays, die als Schnittstelle und „Fenster" zu den unbegrenzten Weiten virtueller Netzwerke fungieren. Das gesamte Gebäude, Innen- und Außenraum, wird so zum Informationsträger. Fast schon wieder ein entgegengesetztes Konzept verfolgt Adam Somlai-Fischer mit Aleph. Nicht die Verfügbarkeit von Informationen für alle steht im Vordergrund, sondern die ganze Welt wird in einem Bild gespiegelt, das gleichzeitig immer nur von einem bestimmten Punkt aus sichtbar ist. Der Prototyp Aleph zählt außerdem zu den mechanischen Medienfassaden, die nicht durch das Aussenden von Licht kommunizieren, sondern bei denen zum Beispiel durch Elektromotoren oder Druckluft Mitteilungen auf der Gebäudeoberfläche generiert werden. Einen ähnlichen Ansatz verfolgt auch das Projekt Flare von WHITEvoid. Bei diesem modularen System können die einzelnen Metallelemente, aus denen sich die Fassade zusammensetzt, mittels Druckluft in unterschiedliche Positionen gekippt werden und dadurch das Sonnenlicht unterschiedlich stark reflektieren. So entsteht eine dynamisch das Gebäude umspielende Hülle. Vielen der Protagonisten sind die Kritikpunkte, die Medienfassaden gegenüber geäußert werden, durchaus bewusst und ein Anlass für die Weiterentwicklung der eigenen Arbeit. Dies zeigt sich bereits in den Vorbehalten gegenüber dem Begriff „Medienfassade", wie sie Tim und Jan Edler von realities:united formulieren:

Über den Begriff Medienfassade sind wir unglücklich, weil er sehr stark geprägt ist. Medienfassade bedeutet häufig: „Ich habe ein Haus – und an einem Stückchen vor dem

conveyor of information. Adam Somlai-Fischer follows on the other hand an almost opposite conception with Aleph. In the foreground is not access to information for all, but rather a mirroring of the entire world in an image that is visible only from a particular position. The Aleph prototype is also among the mechanical media façades, which communicate not by emitting light, but which generate images on the surface of the building by way of electromotors or compressed air pistons. The project Flare by WHITEvoid takes a similar approach. In this modular system the individual metal elements, of which the façade consists, can be tilted into different positions using pressurized air, thereby reflecting sunlight with varying intensity. This produces an envelope that plays dynamically around the building. Many of the protagonists are aware of the points of criticism that have been voiced in respect of media façades, and see these as a provocation to further development of their own work. This is shown in the reservations formuated by Tim and Jan Edler from realities:united in respect of the concept "media façades:"

We are unhappy with the concept media façade, because it seems a very loaded term … media façade often means: "I have a building—and on some little part in front of the building we have hung a television." This widely held definition is too narrow. We thus use other descriptions for our projects, as with the "Communicative Display Skin" at the Kunsthaus Graz[2] or the "Light Media Installation" at Potsdamer Platz[3].

Haus ist jetzt ein Fernseher dran.." Diese land-
läufige Definition finden wir viel zu eng.
Unsere Projekte nennen wir daher alle anders,
etwa „Communicative Display Skin" am Kunsthaus Graz[2] oder „Light Media Installation" am
Potsdamer Platz[3].

Anstatt diese Entwicklung als etwas
Schubladisierbares, vollkommen Neues zu betrachten, geht es uns darum, die Kontinuität zu
betonen: Durch kleine, technische Zufügungen
wird die „normale Architektur" medialisiert
und fängt an, dynamisch zu werden. Wir
begreifen das als einen Prozess, der noch eine
lange Zeit andauern wird − vielleicht wird die
Architektur erst in hundert Jahren tatsächlich
relevante Gestaltung von dynamischen Objekten leisten können. Viele unserer Projekte
handeln daher von Zwischenstationen auf
diesem Weg. (…) Zudem deckt sich ein
großer Teil unseres Interesses gar nicht mit
der Fassade im Sinne einer abgekoppelten
Haut oder Oberfläche. Vielmehr finden wir es
spannend zu überlegen, wie der Ausdruck
aus dem Gebäude, aus der dreidimensionalen
Struktur heraus, entsteht.[4]

Müssen es also immer hochauflösende
High-End-Fassaden sein? Vergleicht man die
Relation zwischen Pixel und Computermonitor,
wie groß ist dann ein einzelner Bildpunkt auf
einem Gebäude? Können Fassadeninstallationen auch in die Tiefe eines Gebäudes
wirken? Und was wäre, wenn man die bereits
vorhandene Gebäudetechnologie, etwa Licht-
technik oder Sonnenschutzsysteme, für die
mediale Bespielung „kidnappen" könnte?
realities:united entwickeln ihre Projekte immer

*Rather than seeing this development as some-
thing entirely new, for us it is about emphasizing
the continuity: through small, technical
additions a "normal architecture" is medialized
and begins to be become dynamic. We see
this as a process that will continue for a long
time yet—perhaps it will take a hundred years
for architecture to really achieve relevant
formation of dynamic objects. Many of our
projects are thus intended as intermediate
stations along this path. … Moreover, much
of our interest is not really in the façade in
the sense of a separate skin or surface. We
find it much more exciting to consider how
expression arises from the building, out of its
three-dimensional structure.[4]*

Do we always need to have high-definition
High-End façades? If we compare the relation
of pixel to computer monitor, how large then
is a single picture element on a building? Can
façade installations also continue into the
depth of a building? And what if one could
"kidnap" already existing building technologies,
such as lighting technology or sun protection
systems for playing the media? realities:united
always develop their projects in relation to the
particular building. With BIX at the Kunsthaus
Graz, for example, they consciously decided on
a low-resolution façade installation, and used
commonly available incandescent lamps, but
were able to light up the entire building surface.
For the new Media Art Museum in Cordoba,
Spain, they experimented with different picture
resolutions in different parts of the façade—
similar to the visual mechanism of the human
eye, which can see sharply only with a small
area of the retina, but can generate a clear

im engen Zusammenhang mit dem jeweiligen Gebäude. Bei BIX am Kunsthaus Graz haben sie sich zum Beispiel bewusst für eine niedrig auflösende Fassadeninstallation aus handels-üblichen Glühlampen entschieden, konnten aber so die gesamte amorphe Gebäudeober-fläche bespielen. Für das neue Medienkunsthaus in Cordoba in Spanien experimentierten sie mit unterschiedlichen Bildauflösungen in ver-schiedenen Bereichen der Fassade – analog zum Sehmechanismus des menschlichen Auges, das auch nur mit einem sehr kleinen Bereich der Netzhaut scharf sieht, aber durch Abtasten eines Gegenstandes in Sekunden-bruchteilen ein klares Bild erzeugen kann. Und bei dem bisher nicht realisierten Projekt NIX wurde die „Sowiesotechnik" eines Hochhauses, also seine funktionale, sowieso vorhandene Infrastruktur, zum Träger eines künstlerischen Ausdrucks weiterentwickelt. Gordon Kipping vom New Yorker Büro G TECTS sieht das Potenzial der Verbindung von Architektur und Technologie durchaus ambivalent, wie er in einem Interview mit plan a äußerte:

Der Grundgedanke ist, dass Gebäudeober-flächen mehr leisten können, als mit Stein oder Holz möglich wäre. Sie könnten Informationen übermitteln und als eine Schnittstelle fungieren, die den Austausch zwischen Menschen oder zwischen Menschen und Informationen unter-stützt. (...) Neue Informationstechnologien haben das Potenzial für radikalere Verände-rungen in der Architektur als der Einzug von Glas als Baumaterial. Diese Technologien können Räume verbinden, die geografisch weit entfernt voneinander liegen, und Wände durchdringen. Sie können uns dabei helfen,

picture by scanning an object in frac-tions of a second. And in the not yet realized project NIX, the "anyhow technologies" of a skyscraper, that is the functional infrastructure that is present in the building anyhow, are further developed as the medium of artistic expression. Gordon Kipping of the New York architecture office G TECTS is ambivalent about the potential connection between architecture and technology, as he makes clear in his interview with plan a:

The basic thought is that building surfaces could do more stone or wood allow. They could communicate information and act as the interface between people and these largely invisible networks. ... Electronic information technologies have the potential to be more radically transformative than glass as an architectural device or material. The techno-logies can connect spaces that are physically distant, it can penetrate a wall or a war. It can aid in the democratization of our built environment and the connection of private and public space. It can also do the opposite. It can increase the exercise of discipline on a people and further isolate and alienate individuals. It all depends on how it is de-ployed, and that is where the architect can be of service.[5]

Could it be that the "current threat" emerges "not only from the advertising and light designers, but also from the fraternity of architects themselves,"[6] all caught up in the "struggle for momentary media attention?"[7] Or is not the current task and challenge for achitects, as "formers of space," to develop

*unsere gebaute Umwelt demokratischer zu
machen – und sie können genau das Gegen-
teil bewirken. Sie können die Unterdrückung
ganzer Völker weiter verschlimmern, genauso
wie die Isolation und Entfremdung einzelner
Individuen. Alles hängt davon ab, wie diese
Technologien ein-gesetzt werden – und an
der Stelle sind es die Architekten, die darauf
Einfluss nehmen können.[5]*

Ist es also so, dass die „aktuelle Bedrohung
(…) nicht nur von den Werbe- und Lichtde-
signern, sondern von der Zunft der Architekten
selbst"[6] ausgeht, alle gefesselt im „Kampf um
die kurzzeitige öffentliche Aufmerksamkeit"[7]?
Oder ist es nicht gerade die Aufgabe und
Herausforderung für Architekten, eine sinnliche,
der Architektur angemessene Sprache für
Medienfassaden zu entwickeln, jenseits rein
ökonomischer Verwertungsinteressen?

*Soll die Stadt mit neuen medialen Ober-
flächen gedacht werden, dann muss für ihre
Ästhetik eine ähnliche verbindliche Zielvor-
stellung entwickelt werden, um ihren Inhalten
eine konstruktive Wirkung zu geben. Das bedeutet, (…) eine klare, verständliche und
übertragbare Sprache mit Vokabel, Syntax und
Grammatik entwickelt werden muss. (…)
[N]eue Medienarchitektur (…) [muss sich]
mit den bestehenden Realitäten verbünden,
sie durchdringen und so neue, stärkere
Wahrnehmungen und Ausdrucksformen der
gebauten Umwelt möglich machen. Hier
liegt das wahre, revolutionäre Potenzial der
Medienarchitektur – sie muss sich dieses
Potenzials nur noch bewusst werden.[8]*

a sense-oriented, architecturally appropriate
language for media façades, beyond the
interests of purely economic utilization?

*If the city is to be thought through with
new media surfaces, then an appropriately
binding objective must be developed for
their aesthetic, so that their contents have a
constructive effect. This means developing
a clear, understandable and transferable
language with vocabulary, syntax and grammar.
… [N]ew media architecture … bound up with
existing realities, must penetrate through them
and thus make possible new, more intensive
perceptions and forms of expression for
the built environment. This is the true, revo-
lutionary potential of media architecture—
it needs only to become conscious of this
potential.[8]*

1 Auszug aus der Antrittsvorlesung, die Hans Stimmann als
Honorarprofessor am Dortmunder Institut für Stadtbaukunst
am 05. Mai 2008 gehalten hat / Excerpt from Hans
Stimmann's inaugural address as honorary professor at the
Dortmund Institute for Urban Planning on May 5, 2008.

2 bezieht sich auf das Projekt / see project BIX

3 bezieht sich auf das Projekt / see project SPOTS

4 Interview realities:united mit / with plan a, 11.02.2009

5 Schriftliches / written interview Gordon Kipping mit /
with plan a, 06.03.2009

6 Hans Stimmann, ebenda / ibid.

7 Hans Stimmann, ebenda / ibid.

8 Auszug aus einem unveröffentlichten Thesenpapier,
das realities:united anlässlich ihrer Publikation „Featuring"
(Arbeitstitel) verfasst haben. / Excerpt from an unpublished
thesis paper produced by realities:united for their publication
"Featuring" (Stand / version: 19.01.2009)

14
Emotional City

D-Tower / NOX Architects (NL) / 2005
Emotional Cities / Erik Kirkortz (SE) / seit / since 2007

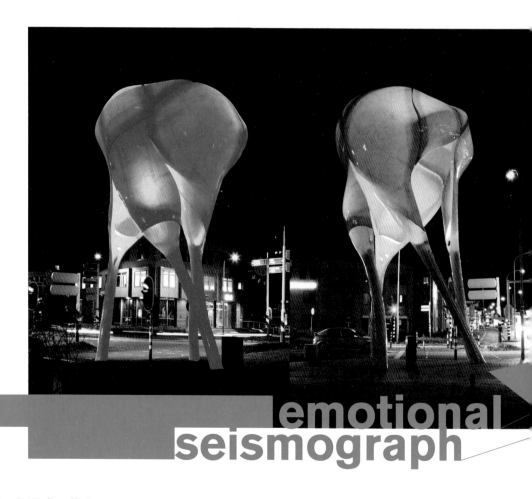

emotional
seismograph

Bei Emotional Cities und **D-Tower** werden Gebäude zum Seismografen der emotionalen Befindlichkeit einer Stadt. Der zwölf Meter hohe, an einen Organismus erinnernde Turm, von Lars Spybroek (NOX) für die niederländische Gemeinde Doetinchem entworfen, ändert entsprechend der Stimmung der Einwohner seine Farbe. Die Doetinchemer können über eine Webseite einen Fragebogen zu ihrer aktuellen Befindlichkeit ausfüllen. Daraus wird dann in einer Art „Tagesauswertung" ein Mittelwert berechnet und der Turm verändert seine Farbe: Blau steht für Glück, Gelb für Angst oder Grün für Hass.

With Emotional Cities and **D-Tower**, buildings become seismographs of the emotional state of a city. The twelve-meter-high, organism-like tower of Lars Spybroek (NOX), designed for the Dutch municipalty of Doetinchem, changes color in accordance with the mood of the inhabitants. The people of Doetinchem can fill out a website questionaire on their current emotional state. From this a kind of "daily assessment" is made, an average value is calculated, and the tower changes its color: blue is for happiness, yellow for fear, green for hate.

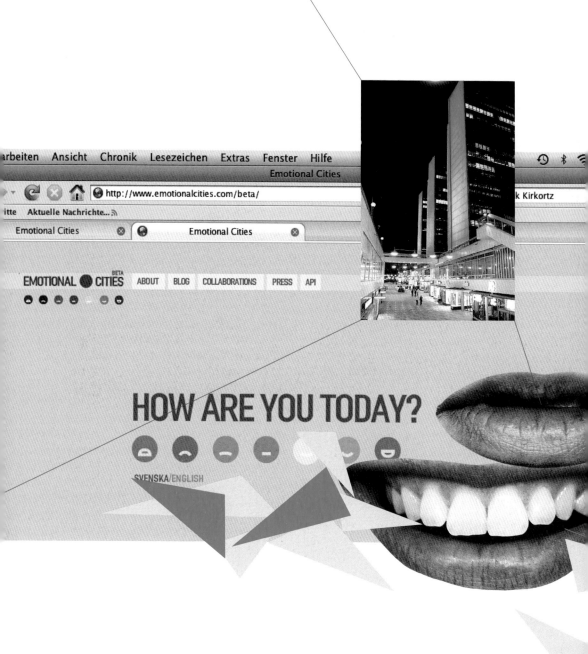

Auf einem ähnlichen Prinzip beruht auch **Emotional Cities**: Hier kann jeder tagesaktuell auf dem Onlineportal www.emotionalcities.com seine Stimmung registrieren – zur Auswahl stehen sieben farbige Icons von „Rot" (für glücklich) bis „Violett" (für traurig). Das Portal ist ganzjährig aktiv und versammelt Daten zur emotionalen Befindlichkeit von Nutzern aus über zwanzig Städten weltweit. Im physischen Raum materialisiert wird seit 2007 – zumindest temporär – die Stimmung der Stockholmer. Aus ihren abgegebenen Stimmungen wird ein Mittelwert errechnet und stündlich aktualisiert auf fünf LED-Fassaden auf das Hötorget-Hochhaus im Zentrum Stockholms übertragen. Die leuchten dann – je nach Stimmungslage der Stockholmer – in gelb, grün, blau, orange oder eben rot. Die Installation war im Jahr 2007 und 2008 jeweils für drei Monate in Stockholm zu sehen. Eine ähnliche Aktion gab es außerdem in Seoul in Kooperation mit dem Art Center Nabi. Der Initiator Erik Kirkortz plant Installationen in weiteren europäischen Städten.

How are you today?

Emotional Cities is based on a similar principle: it allows everyone to register a daily update of their mood on the online portal www.emotionalcities.com—there is a choice of seven colored icons from "red" (for happy) through to "violet" (for sad). The portal is active all year and collects data on the emotional states of users from over 20 cities around the world. Since 2007 there has been a materialization in physical space—at least temporarily—of the mood of the Stockholmers. An average value is generated from their registered moods and updated hourly on five LED-façades on the Hötorget-Building in the center of Stockholm. They then light up—depending on the mood of the Stockholmers—in yellow, green, blue, orange, or red. The installation was shown for three months in 2007 and in 2008 in Stockholm. A similar action was also presented in Seoul in cooperation with the Art Center Nabi. Erik Kirkortz, the initiator, is planning installations in other European cities.

15
Big Brother?

Grandes Lignes / HeHe (FR / UK / GER) / 2007
Mojo / Christian Moeller (GER / USA) / 2007
Nosy / Christian Moeller (GER / USA) / 2007

Diese Installation des in Paris ansässigen Künstlerduos HeHe spart nicht nur Energie – sie hebt den Einzelnen aus der anonymen Masse hervor und begleitet ihn ein Stück seines Weges. **Grandes Lignes** ist ein reaktives Lichtsystem, das temporär in eine existierende Fußgängerbrücke in Luxemburg integriert wurde. Die Brücke wird nur beleuchtet, wenn jemand über sie hinübergeht – ein Lichtkegel begleitet den Passanten. Die Installation nimmt Bezug auf das Thema „Migration", mit dem sich Luxemburg als Kulturhauptstadt 2007 unter anderem auseinandergesetzt hat. Migration ist von Verlassen und Ankommen und der Strecke zwischen diesen beiden Punkten gekennzeichnet. „Entlang dieser Strecke trägt jeder seine eigene Geschichte, seinen individuellen kulturellen Hintergrund mit sich", so HeHe – in der Installation Grand Lignes wird das durch die persönliche Lichtsphäre symbolisiert, die den Passanten begleitet, wenn er von einem Ende der Brücke zum anderen läuft.

This installation by the Paris-based artist duo HeHe doesn't just save energy – it lifts the individual out of the anonymous crowd and accompanies them along part of their way. **Grandes Lignes** is a reactive light system that has been temporarily integrated into an existing pedestrian bridge in Luxembourg. The bridge is illuminated only when someone crosses it—a cone of light accompanies the pedestrian. The installation deals with "migration," one of the themes of Luxembourg's year as Cultural Capital 2007. Migration is distinguished by departure, arrival, and by the path in between. "Along this path we each carry our own history, our individual cultural background with us," according to HeHe. In the installation Grandes Lignes **this is symbolized by the personal light sphere that accompanies the passer-by as they walk from one end of the bridge to the other.**

Mojo und Nosy gehören zu einer wachsenden Familie „robotischer Skulpturen", die der Künstler Christian Moeller für öffentliche Plätze in den USA und Asien gestaltet hat. An diesen Skulpturen kommt niemand vorbei, ohne sie zu bemerken. Man könnte Mojo und Nosy als neugierig beschreiben oder aber als aufdringlich. Sie interagieren mit ihrer Umgebung und damit auch mit den Passanten, die plötzlich – gewollt oder ungewollt – in Szene gesetzt werden. **Mojo** wurde 2007 an einer Straßenecke in Los Angeles errichtet. Am Arm des Roboters ist ein Scheinwerfer befestigt, der vorübergehende Passanten verfolgt und für kurze Zeit ins Spotlight der Aufmerksamkeit stellt. Die Szenerie wird von zwei Kameras beobachtet, die auf dem Dach eines benachbarten Gebäudes installiert sind.

Moeller beschreibt seine Arbeiten als satirische Statements zu dem oftmals sterilen, stereotypen und roboterartigen Verhalten von Behörden und Institutionen, die wenig Raum für Freiheit und unabhängige Gedanken lassen. Er kritisiert damit auch die Omnipräsenz von Überwachung im öffentlichen Raum. Andererseits stoppen Nosy und Mojo unseren „Alltagstrott", lassen uns möglicherweise für einen kurzen Moment innehalten und mit den beiden Robotern und ihrer Aufmerksamkeit „spielen".

Mojo and Nosy belong to a growing family of "robotic sculptures", designed by artist Christian Moeller for public spaces in the USA and Asia. No one passes by these sculptures without noticing them. One could describe Mojo and Nosy as inquisitive or as obtrusive. They interact with their surroundings and thereby also with passers-by, who are suddenly—whether they want to be or not—made the center of attention. **Mojo** was set up on a street corner in Los Angeles in 2007. Attached to the arm of the robot is a floodlight that follows passing pedestrians and briefly puts them literally in the spotlight. Two cameras installed on the roof of a neighboring building observe the scene.

Moeller describes his works as satirical statements on the often sterile, stereotyped, and robotlike behavior of authorities and institutions, which leave little room for freedom and independent thought. He also critiques the omnipresence of surveillance in public spaces. On the other hand, Nosy and Mojo interrupt our "everyday routine," allowing us to perhaps reflect for a moment and to "play" with the robots and their attention.

Nosy (englisch für neugierig, fast schon aufdringlich) macht seinem Namen alle Ehre: Die Kamera, die an einem Stahlpfosten an einer Straße Osaki-Citys, einem Tokioter Stadtteil, installiert wurde, beobachtet vorbeilaufende Menschen nicht nur. Sie hebt sie – im wahrsten Sinne des Wortes – weithin sichtbar aus der Masse heraus. Die von der Kamera aufgenommenen Bilder werden als überlebensgroße, grobauflösende Grafiken auf eine LED-Medienfassade übertragen. So schaut man plötzlich überrascht, erfreut, vielleicht aber auch verstört in das eigene Gesicht, das einem von dem 13,5 Meter hohen Turm in der Nachbarschaft entgegen starrt, lächelt, zwinkert …

Nosy lives up to its name: the camera, installed on a steel post on a street in Osaki-City, a district of Tokyo, doesn't just observe passers-by. It lifts them up—in the truest sense of the word—visibly out of the crowd. The pictures taken by the camera are transmitted as larger than lifesized, low-resolution images onto an LED media façade. One is thus suddenly suprised, delighted, but perhaps also bewildered, to see one's own face staring down from a 13.5-meter-high tower …

Spotlight

Überwachung und Sichtbarmachung
Surveillance and Visibility

Christian Moellers Mojo setzt Passanten ins Scheinwerferlicht, lässt die sonst versteckte Beobachtung im urbanen Raum sichtbar und unmittelbar erfahrbar werden. Dabei wirken seine robotischen Skupturen eher harmlos, fast comichaft überzeichnet in ihrem quietschen-den Rot und entschärfen damit gleichzeitig die Situation: „Ich will doch nur spielen." Auch andere Interventionsprojekte von Künstlern, Architekten und Planern, die sich mit der verbreitetesten Technologie im öffentlichen Raum – der Überwachungstechnologie[1] – beschäftigen, setzen oftmals spielerisch-ironische Statements. Von den New Yorker Surveillance Camera Players, die seit 1996 Theaterstücke vor Überwachungskameras aufführen, bis hin zu den Münchner Urbanau-ten, die bei ihrem Projekt „lausch.angriff" im November 2008 Menschen auf öffentlichen Plätzen nicht nur beobachteten, sondern sie über einen Lautsprecher auch zurechtwiesen: „Nehmen Sie bitte Ihren Hund an die Leine! Das freie Herumlaufen von Hunden ist nicht gestattet." Ironie der Geschichte – was in München als Parodie läuft, ist im britischen

Christian Moeller's Mojo puts passers-by in the spotlight, thus allowing observation, which is usally hidden in urban space, to become visible and immediately experienceable. At the same time, his robotic sculptures seem harmless and almost comically exaggerated in their squeaky red, thus disarming the situation: "I only want to play." Other intervention projects by artists, architects, and planners dealing with the most prevalent technology in public space—surveillance technology[1]— often also make playful-ironic statements. From the New York Surveillance Camera Players, who since 1996 have been performing theater pieces in front of surveillance cameras, to the Munich-based Urbanauten, who with their project "lausch. angriff" in November 2008 not only observed people in public spaces, but issued commands at them over loudspeakers: "Put your dog on its leash! Dogs are not permitted off leash in this park." The irony of the story is that what in Munich is performed as parody is in British Middlesbrough already reality: here, seven of the 158 municipal surveillance cameras are fitted with loudspeakers against "antisocial

Middlesbrough bereits Realität: Hier sind sieben der 158 städtischen Überwachungskameras mit Lautsprechern gegen „antisoziales Verhalten" ausgestattet. Big Brother lässt grüßen.

Dieser immer massivere Einsatz von Überwachungstechnologie im öffentlichen Raum wird uns durch Projekte wie Mojo und Nosy exemplarisch vorgeführt. Diese Inter-ventionen geben uns aber andererseits auch die Möglichkeit, unsere Präsenz im öffentlichen Raum für einen Moment lang aus der Masse herauszuheben – also bewusst mit dem Beobachtetsein zu spielen, uns zu exhibitionieren. Die Sehnsucht, von den anderen gesehen, wahrgenommen zu werden, ist alt. Pathetisch hat sie Alfred Wolfenstein vor fast einhundert Jahren in seinem expressionistischen Großstadtgedicht „Städter" formuliert, das er mit den Zeilen „Dicht wie die Löcher eines Siebes stehn / Fenster beieinander, drängend fassen / Häuser sich so dicht an, daß die Straßen / Grau geschwollen wie Gewürgte stehn" beginnen und wie folgt enden lässt: „Ganz unangerührt und ungeschaut / Steht ein jeder fern und fühlt: alleine."

Wahrgenommen zu werden, Spuren im Raum zu hinterlassen, die (vielleicht oftmals bewusst gesuchte, aber eben auch manchmal erdrückende) Anonymität der Großstadt zu verlassen, sich sichtbar zu machen – all das sind Bedürfnisse, die durch die Verbindung von Architektur und Technologie im öffentlichen Raum erfüllt werden könnten. Die Medienwissenschaftlerin Miriam Struppek hat dieses Potenzial in ihrer Arbeit „Interaktions-

behavior." Big Brother sends his regards. This ever greater application of surveillance technology in public space is demonstrated in an exemplary way by projects like Mojo and Nosy.

But these interventions also give us the opportunity to momentarily lift our public presence out of the crowd—to consciously play with being observed, to be exhibitionist. The desire to be seen, to be taken notice of by others, is old. Almost a hundred years ago, Alfred Wolfenstein gave an emotive formulation of this desire in his expressionist big-city poem "Städter," which begins: "Close as the holes of a sieve stand / Windows tight together, crowding houses / Clutch themselves so close, that the streets / Swollen gray stand as if strangled." It ends with the lines: "Entirely untouched and unseen / Each stands apart and feels: alone."

To be noticed, to leave traces in space, to escape the (perhaps often consciously sought, but then sometimes overwhelming) anonymity of big city, to make oneself visible—these are needs that can be met by bringing together architecture and technology in public space. The media theorist Miriam Struppek has examined this potential in her work "Interaction Field—Public Space,"[2] to show "how new media can be used in an alternative way, to use new qualities of interaction to contribute to a reactivation of an integrated and identity-founding city space for a democratic society." The installations may thus contribute to "confrontation free of fear, and contact with strangers," to "formation of the public sphere through critique, discussion, and reflection on

feld – öffentlicher Raum"[2] untersucht, um aufzuzeigen „wie die Neuen Medien alternativ genutzt werden können, um durch neue Interaktionsqualitäten zur Reaktivierung eines integrierenden und identitätsstiftenden Stadtraums für eine demokratische Gesellschaft beizutragen." So könnten die Installationen zur „angstfreien Konfrontation und zum Kontakt mit Fremden" beitragen, „Öffentlichkeitsbildung durch Kritik, Diskussion und Reflexion der Gesellschaft" sowie „soziale Interaktion und Verortung in der lokalen Nachbarschaft" fördern und zur „bewussten Teilnahme an der Gestaltung des öffentlichen Raums" animieren. Die in diesem Kapitel vorgestellten Projekte D-Tower und Emotional Cities könnte man vor allem im Sinne der beiden letztgenannten Punkte verstehen. Die Bewohner der niederländischen Gemeinde Doetinchem und die Einwohner Stockholms erfahren durch die Installationen etwas über die Befindlichkeit ihrer Nachbarn und nehmen selbst Einfluss auf die (Licht-)Gestaltung eines markanten Gebäudes ihres Umfeldes.

Ein anderes Beispiel ist das Projekt Blinkenlights[3] des Chaos Computer Clubs, das 2001 mit der Bespielung der Fassade am Haus des Lehrers am Berliner Alexanderplatz begann und seine Fortsetzung mit „Arcade" an der Nationalbibliothek Paris (2002) und jüngst am Rathaus Toronto mit „Stereoscape" fand. Über ihre Mobiltelefone können Passanten Einfluss auf die Lichtinstallation nehmen, gemeinsam Computerspiele spielen und eigene Filme gestalten und auf der Medienfassade abspielen.

society" as well as promoting "social interaction and rootedness in the local neighborhood," and animating people to a "conscious participation in the shaping of public space." Two of the projects presented in this chapter, D-Tower and Emotional Cities, could be understood above all in terms of the last two points. The inhabitants of the Dutch municipalty of Doetinchem and the residents of Stockholm discover through the installations something of the emotional state of their neighbors, and have an influence on the (lighting-)appearance of a prominent building in their surrounding area.

Another example is the project Blinkenlights[3] of the Chaos Computer Club, which began in 2001 with an installation on the façade of the Haus des Lehrers at Berlin Alexanderplatz, and was continued with "Arcade" at the National Library of Paris (2002), and most recently with "Stereoscape" at the Town Hall in Toronto. Passers-by could use their mobile phones to influence the light installations, play computer games together, and create films to be played on the media façades.

The following projects, with which the chapter PUBLIC (ATMO)SPHERE ends, show a different sensuous potential of the integration of technology and public space. Here it is not so much about making the individual visible, or about interpersonal interaction or communication. At issue, rather, is visualization in the sense of making otherwise unseen phenomena visible. The interdisciplinary collective doubleNegative Architecture creates spatial structures on the basis of data collected from the physical surroundings of a building:

Die im folgenden vorgestellten Projekte, die das Kapitel PUBLIC (ATMO)SPHERE beschließen, zeigen ein weiteres, sinnliches Potenzial der Integration von Technologie und öffentlichem Raum auf. Hier geht es weniger um das Sichtbarwerden des Einzelnen oder um zwischenmenschliche Interaktion oder Kommunikation. Vielmehr geht es um die Visualisierung, die Sichtbarmachung sonst unsichtbarer Phänomene. Das interdisziplinäre Kollektiv doubleNegative Architecture erschafft räumliche Strukturen basierend auf Daten aus der physischen Umgebung eines Gebäudes: Windgeschwindigkeit, Temperatur und Lautstärke werden zu raumdefinierenden Größen und als sich ständig verändernder architektonischer Organismus visualisiert. Der britische Architekt und Designer Jason Bruges verwandelt Wind zu Licht und schafft so eine ephemere Architektur im Stadtraum. Und das Künstlerduo HeHe benutzt schließlich die Emissionsschwaden eines Kraftwerks als Projektionsleinwand, um den Energieverbrauch eines Stadtteils von Helsinki abzubilden.

wind velocity, temperature, and sound intensity are turned into space-defining quantities and visualized as a continually mutating architectural organism. The British architect and designer Jason Bruges converts wind into light to create an ephemeral architecture within the city. And finally, the artist duo HeHe uses the emission vapors of a power plant as a projection screen, to depict the energy use of a Helsinki district.

1 Nach Schätzungen gibt es derzeit in Deutschland circa 400.000 Überwachungskameras. / According to estimates, there are about 400,000 surveillance cameras in Germany.

2 Vgl. / see www.interactionfield.de

3 Weitere Informationen unter / Furhter information at www.blinkenlights.net

16
Invisibles

Corpora Insi(gh)te / doubleNegatives Architecture (JP / HU / CH)
seit / since 2007
Nuage Vert / HeHe (FR / UK / GER) / 2008

k

Corpora in Si(gh)te ist ein „digitales Nervensystem", ein architektonischer Körper im virtuellen Raum, dessen Gestalt durch Daten aus der physischen Umwelt bestimmt wird. Hier wird Unsichtbares in räumlichen Strukturen visualisiert. Corpora in Si(gh)te ist eine experimentelle Installation, die das interdisziplinäre Team von doubleNegatives Architecture (dNA) bisher im Yamaguchi Center for Art, auf der 11. Architekturbiennale Venedig und im Rahmen der 9. Transmediale im Collegium Hungaricum Berlin gezeigt hat. Auf den Gebäuden der Ausstellungsräume wurden jeweils Sensoren installiert, die die physikalischen Daten der Umgebung aufnehmen: Temperatur, Windrichtung, Geräusche und Lichtverhältnisse. Die gesammelten Daten werden von einer Software übersetzt und in virtuelle Netzstrukturen umgewandelt. Wie ein Organismus verändert sich Corpora entsprechend den aufgenommenen Reizen aus der Umgebung. Bei der Eröffnung der Installation im Collegium Hungaricum zog die Struktur sich plötzlich ganz zurück – die Zuschauer applaudierten zu heftig …

Corpora in Si(gh)te is a "digital nervous system," an architectural body in virtual space, whose shape is determined by data from the physical environment. Here the invisible is visualized in spatial structures. Corpora in Si(gh)te is an experimental installation that the interdisciplinary team from doubleNegatives Architecture (dNA) has so far presented in the Yamaguchi Center for Art, at the 11th Architecture Biennale in Venice, and at the Collegium Hungaricum Berlin as part of the 9th Transmediale. Sensors are installed on the buildings of the installation spaces, and produce information about the surroundings: temperature, wind direction, sounds, and light conditions. Software translates this data and converts it into virtual mesh constructions. Like an organism, Corpora changes in accordance with stimuli from its surroundings. At the opening of the installation in Collegium Hungaricum the structure suddenly withdrew into itself—the spectators applauded too loudly …

Bei dieser Installation wurde der Himmel über Ruoholahti bei Helsinki zur Leinwand: In die Emissionsschwaden des örtlichen Kraftwerks projizierten die Künstler Helen Evans und Heiko Hansen (HeHe) zwei Wochen lang eine grüne Wolke, die sich proportional zum Energieverbrauch der Einwohner veränderte. **Nuage Vert** ist Teil der „Pollstream Series". Im Rahmen dieser Projektserie geht es darum, den Verbrauch von Energieressourcen und Umweltverschmutzung zeitgleich zu ihrem Entstehen im öffentlichen Raum zu visualisieren. Für Nuage Vert installierten HeHe eine wärmesensible Kamera, einen Computer mit Internetverbindung und ein Lasergerät auf einem dem Kraftwerk gegenüberliegenden Gebäude. Die Kamera lokalisierte die Rauchschwaden, der Rechner wurde mit aktuellen Stromverbrauchsdaten aus der Umgebung versorgt und berechnete daraus die Form der Wolke, die dann mit dem Projektor als grüne Laserkontur in den Himmel bzw. in die Kraftwerksabgase projiziert wurde. Die Aktion wurde von einer umfangreichen Medienkampagne begleitet, um die Einwohner von Ruoholahti zur Energieeinsparung zu animieren.

This installation turned the sky over Ruoholahti near Helsinki into a projection screen: For two weeks, the artists Helen Evans and Heiko Hansen (HeHe) projected onto the emission vapors of the local power station a green cloud whose size varied proportionally to the energy use of the residents. **Nuage Vert** is part of the "Pollstream Series." This series is about creating a visualization in public space of energy use and pollution at the time when they are occurring. For Nuage Vert, HeHe installed a heat-sensitive camera, a computer with an internet connection and a laser device on a building facing the power station. The camera located the steam emissions, the computer was fed current data on electricity use in the surrounding area and then calculated on the basis of these the shape of the cloud, which was then projected as a green laser contour onto the sky or onto exhaust gases of the power station. The action was accompanied by an extensive media campaign, to engage the residents of Ruoholahti in saving energy.

17
(Open) Air Architecture

Wind to Light / Jason Bruges Studio (UK) / 2007
Aeolian Tower / Jason Bruges Studio (UK) / 2008

Wie eine grün und blau schimmernde Wolke schwebt die Installation von Jason Bruges über dem Southbank Centre in London. **Wind to Light** besteht aus hunderten von kleinen Modulen: Turbinen im Miniaturformat, die direkt an LEDs gekoppelt sind. Angetrieben durch den Wind, erzeugen sie Strom und bringen so die LEDs zum Leuchten. Die einzelnen Module sind auf schlanken, 1,8 Meter hohen Stäben befestigt und schwingen sanft im Wind.wurde als ortsbezogene, temporäre Installation im Rahmen der britischen Architekturwoche 2007 entwickelt. Unter dem übergreifenden Motto „How green is our space?" lag der Fokus auf den Themen Nachhaltigkeit und Klimawandel. Bruges verzichtet darauf, mahnend den Zeigefinger zu erheben. Seine Antwort besticht durch ihre sublime Poesie: Wind to Light verbraucht nur so viel Energie, wie durch den Wind erzeugt werden kann. Gleichzeitig wird die – per se unsichtbare – Windenergie zum visuellen Gestaltungsmittel und transformiert das Southbank Center zum „Sensing Space". Je nach Windstärke leuchtet Wind to Light als ephemere Erweiterung des Gebäudes in unterschiedlicher Intensität auf.

Like a green and blue shimmering cloud, the installation of Jason Bruges hovers over the Southbank Centre in London. **Wind to Light** consists of hundreds of small modules: turbines in miniature format, directly coupled to LEDs. Powered by the wind, they produce electricity and thus cause the LEDs to light up. The single modules are attached to slender, 1.8 meter high rods, and swing gently in the wind. Wind to light was developed as a site-specific, temporary installation for British Architecture Week 2007. Under the general motto "How green is our space?," the focus was on the themes of sustainability and climate change. Bruges avoids shaking his finger admonishingly. His answer persuades rather with its sublime poetry: Wind to Light uses only as much energy as can be made with the wind. At the same time, the—per se invisible—wind energy becomes a medium of visual formation, and transforms the Southbank Centre into a "sensing space," Depending on the strength of the wind, Wind to Light lights up in variable intensity as an ephemeral extension to the building.

Aeolian Tower könnte man als zeitgenössische Fortschreibung von Toyo Itos berühm-
tem Turm der Winde (siehe S. 70) verstehen.
Die Installation war Teil des „onedotzero_
adventures in motion" Festivals am British Film
Institute (BFI) in London im November 2008.
Rot glühte der 15 Meter hohe Turm, dessen
Name auf den griechischen Gott des Windes
Aiolos verweist, neben der Londoner Waterloo
Bridge. Ähnlich dem Prinzip von Wind to Light
wurde ein Stahlträger mit einer „Haut" aus
1200 windgetriebenen Turbinen-LED-Modulen
eingekleidet. Wirbelnde Lichtmuster machten
die Intensität und Richtung der Böen sichtbar.
Ab einer Windstärke von drei mph erstrahlten
die LEDs in ihrer ganzen Helligkeit. In einem
weiteren Testaufbau wurden zudem alle auf
einem Panel montierten LEDs einzeln via
Computer gesteuert. Dadurch konnten grobauflösende Bild- und Textbotschaften übermittelt
werden. Denkbar ist hier die Weiterentwicklung
zu einem auch für kommerzielle Zwecke einsetz-
baren, windgetriebenen Display, dessen Betrieb
keine zusätzliche Energie verbrauchen würde.

Aeolian Tower could be understood as
a contemporary further development of Toyo
Itos famous Tower of Winds (see p. 70).
The installation was part of the "onedotzero_
adventures in motion" festival at the British
Film Institute (BFI) in London in November
2008. The fifteen-meter-high tower, named
after the Greek god of wind Aeolus, glowed
red next to the London Waterloo Bridge.
Using a principle similar to that of Wind to
Light, a steel construction was wrapped in
a "skin" of 1200 wind-powered Turbine-LED-
modules. Swirling light patterns made the
intensity and direction of the wind gusts
visible. By a wind velocity of over three mph
the LEDs shone with their full intensity. In
another test setup, all of the LEDs mounted
on a panel were individually controlled by
computer. It was thereby possible to display
low-resolution pictures and text-messages.
This could conceivably allow the further
development of a wind-powered display
for commercial uses that would require no
external energy.

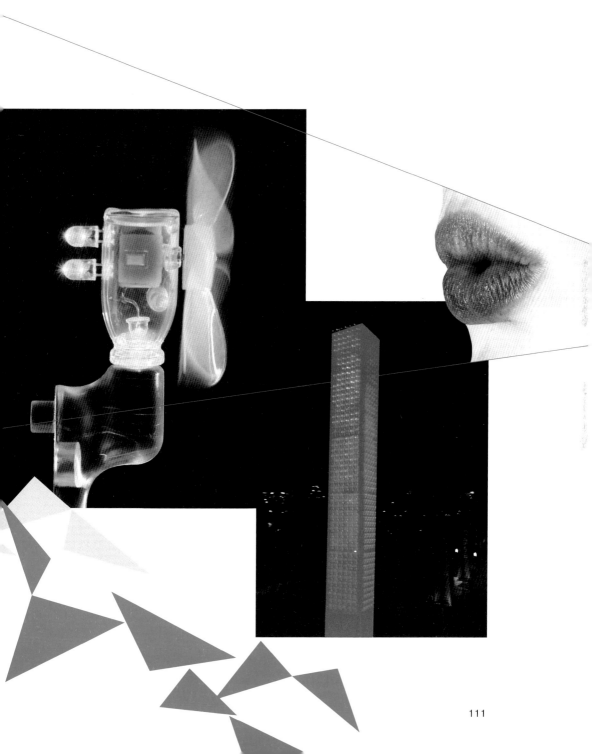

111

III.
INTERACTIVE
FUTURE
Raum im Zeichen von Interaktivität
Space under the Sign of Interactivity

Müsste ein im wahrsten Sinne des Wortes „Sensing Space", ein wahrnehmender Raum, nicht zwangsläufig ein unerwartetes Verhalten zeigen, frei von zuvor festgelegten Mustern und externer Kontrolle? Ein sich ständig neu definierender Organismus, der in der Lage ist, zu lernen und uns immer wieder zu überraschen oder aber ein Raum, der sich grenzenlos von seinen Nutzern gestalten lässt? Was genau bedeutet Interaktivität – ein Begriff, der im Zusammenhang mit Architektur vielleicht viel zu schnell und wie ein Etikett verwendet wird – wenn man dieses Prinzip in all seiner Konsequenz auf physische und virtuelle Räume überträgt? Welche Möglichkeiten eröffnen neue Technologien, um das, was Visionäre wie Cedric Price mit Fun Palace oder Constant Nieuwenhuys mit New Babylon einst erdachten, umzusetzen beziehungsweise weiterzuentwickeln? Inwieweit lässt sich der Open-Source-Gedanke auch auf die Architektur übertragen?

In den vorangegangenen Kapiteln wurden bereits einige dieser Fragestellungen angeschnitten. INTERACTIVE FUTURE stellt nun explizit Forschungsprojekte und Experimente vor, bei denen Architekten, Programmierer und Wissenschaftler die Bedeutung verschiedener Konzepte von Interaktivität und der daraus entstehenden Potenziale für die Schaffung von Räumen und die Rolle der Nutzer bzw. Bewohner untersuchen. Einige Projekte bewegen sich dabei (noch) auf der Ebene der Grundlagenforschung, für andere sind zukünftige Anwendungen auch im Bereich der Architektur bereits offensichtlich. INTERACTIVE FUTURE beschließt „Sensing Space" und eröffnet zugleich Felder der zukünftigen Auseinandersetzung.

Wouldn't a "sensing space" in the truest sense of the word inevitably have to show unexpected behavior, free from predetermined patterns and external control? An organism ever defining itself anew, capable of learning, and of surprising us again and again, or else a space that allows itself to be limitlessly determined by its users? What exactly is the meaning of interactivity—a concept perhaps much too quickly brought into connection with architecture, and applied like a label—when we apply this principle with all of its consequences to physical and virtual spaces? What possibilities do new technologies open up for putting into practice or further developing the ideas laid out by visionaries like Cedric Price in Fun Palace or Constant Nieuwenhuys with New Babylon? To what extent can the Open-Source-Idea be applied to architecture?

Many of these questions have already been introduced in previous chapters. INTERACTIVE FUTURE explicitly presents research projects and experiments in which architects, programmers, and scientists investigate the significance of different conceptions of interactivity and the resulting potential for the creation of spaces and for the role of the user or inhabitant. Some of the projects are still (so far) at the stage of basic research; in other cases, future applications, including in the realm of architecture, are already in view. INTERACTIVE FUTURE concludes "Sensing Space" and at the same time opens up fields for future examination.

18
Interaction Pioneer

Fun Palace / Cedric Price (UK) / Entwurf / Design 1961
Inter-Action Centre / Cedric Price (UK) / 1972

Als ein „Kit of Parts" – eine Art Bausatz, dessen einzelne Teile durch die Nutzer selbst immer wieder neu kombiniert werden können – bezeichnete Cedric Price seinen **Fun Palace** und ist damit bis heute Pionier und Vorbild für viele „Interaction Architects". Von 1961 bis 1972 arbeitet er am Konzept eines alternativen Bildungs- und Freizeitzentrums. Realisiert wurde es nie. In den technologiegläubigen 1960ern ging man davon aus, dass Maschinen den Menschen immer mehr Arbeit abnehmen und die Arbeitszeiten sich immer weiter verkürzen würden. Der kreative Umgang mit Freizeit wurde zu einem wirtschaftlichen, politischen und sozialen Thema. Auch in der Architektur suchte man nach Antworten auf das „Age of Leisure" und der Fun Palace traf den Nerv der Zeit. Er war radikal in seiner Verbindung von Architektur und Technologie. Eine fixe Form gab es nicht – sie sollte erst aus den jeweiligen Aktivitäten entstehen und sich beständig ändern. Vorgesehen waren Kinos, Labore für wissenschaftliche Experimente, Cafés, Studios für

A "Kit of Parts" whose individual pieces can be set into ever new combinations by the users—this is how Cedric Price described his **Fun Palace**, for which he is still considered a pioneer and model for many "interaction architects." From 1961 to 1972 he worked on the concept of an alternative education and leisure center. It was never built. In the 1960s there were great hopes for technology, and it was assumed that machines would relieve people of increasingly more work, and that working hours would become ever shorter. A creative approach to free time became an economic, political, and social issue. In architecture as well, one was seeking answers for the "age of leisure," and the Fun Palace captured the spirit of the times. It was radical in its combination of architecture and technology. It had no fixed form — it was to come into being only out of particular activities, and then alter itself continually.

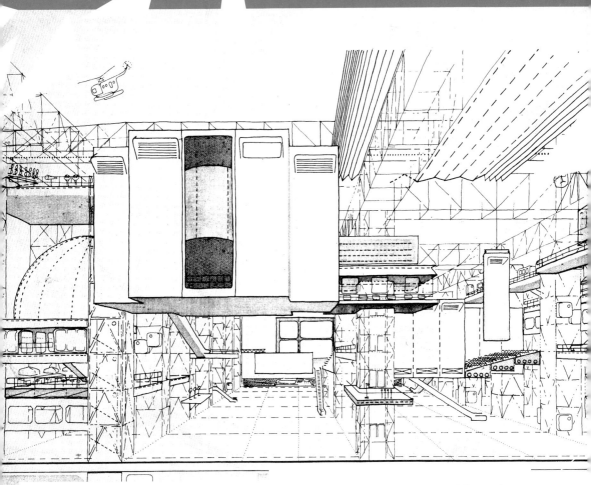

Malerei und Musik etc. In über 400 Zeichnungen, Zeitplänen, Bewegungsdiagrammen und technischen Details entwickelte Price diese „University of the Streets". Teilweise umsetzen konnte er sie einige Jahre später mit dem Inter-Action Centre.

It was planned to include cinemas, laboratories for scientific experiments, cafés, studios for painting, music etc., Price developed this "university of the streets" in over 400 drawings, timeplans, movement diagrams, and technical details. He was able to partially realize them some years later with the Inter-Action Centre.

Das **Inter-Action Centre** führt die Ideen des Fun Palace fort. Konzipiert als „urbane Farm", Selbsthilfezentrum und „lokaler Klub" war es offen für alle Anwohner im Londoner Stadtteil Camden. So gab es unter anderem eine Theater- und Konzertbühne, einen großen Versammlungssaal, eine Bar, einen Jugendclub sowie Kurse zu verschiedenen künstlerischen Aktivitäten. Price verzichtete auf jegliche repräsentative Geste – das Inter Action Centre strahlte eher den Charme einer Containersiedlung aus. In einen doppelgeschossigen, auf einer Betonplatte montierten Stahlrahmenbau wurden entsprechend dem „Plug-in-Prinzip" Geschossplatten, Treppen, Containerelemente etc. eingehängt, deren Konfiguration mit geringem Aufwand immer wieder verändert werden konnte. Die gesamte Konstruktion war auf größtmögliche Flexibilität ausgerichtet – die konsequente Umsetzung von Prices Idee von Kultur und Gesellschaft in beständigem Wandel. Doch nicht nur die konkrete Form war nebensächlich, auch die Lebensdauer des Gebäudes war von Anfang an begrenzt. Bereits mit dem Bau entwickelte Price die Pläne für die Demontage. 2001 wurde das Inter-Action Centre abgerissen.

The **Inter-Action Centre** further develops the ideas of the Fun Palace. Conceived as an "urban farm," self-help center and "local club", it was open for all residents of the London district of Camden. It had, among other things, a stage for theater and concerts, a large meeting hall, a bar, a youth club, and courses in various artistic activities. Price dispensed with all representational gestures—the Inter Action Centre exuded rather the charm of a container settlement. Floor slabs, staircases, container elements, etc., were inserted by "plug-in-principle" into a two-story steel-frame structure built on a concrete slab, and their configuration could be altered again and again with little effort. The entire construction was oriented towards maximum flexibility— the logical realization of Price's idea of culture and society in constant change. But not only was its concrete form secondary, the lifetime of the building was also restricted from the beginning. Already during construction, Price developed the plans for its dismantling. In 2001, the Inter-Action Center was demolished.

plug in
the space
you
need

121,5mm   ⑦ Price

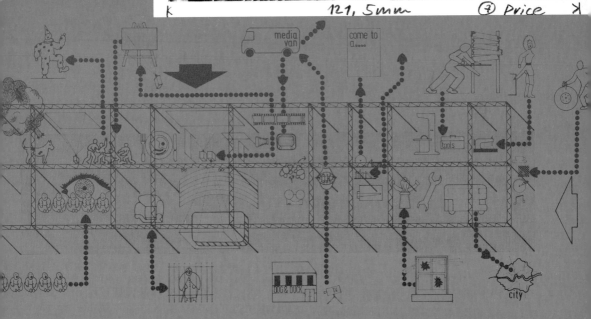

Response!

Was heißt hier eigentlich „interaktiv"?
What does "interactive" really mean here?

Fun Palace und Inter Action Centre, die visionären Projekte des Interaction-Pioniers Cedric Price, waren zunächst nichts weiter als „Skelette" – statisch notwendige und eine einfache Erschließung gewährleistende Grundstrukturen, die erst noch mit „Inhalten" gefüllt werden mussten. Das maßgebliche Prinzip von Price beruhte jeweils darauf, dass ein Gebäude nur durch die Interaktion mit den Menschen, die es nutzen würden, entstehen und sich zudem permanent ändern und neuen Nutzungsanforderungen anpassen würde. Treffen Architektur und neue Technologien aufeinander, werden häufig auch Schlagwörter wie „interaktive Räume", „intelligente Architekturen" oder „responsive environments" bemüht. Doch welche Konzepte stecken genau dahinter? Welche Wechselwirkung findet zwischen uns und den als „intelligent" bezeichneten Objekten oder Architekturen statt? Bedeutet das, dass Räume zukünftig ein eigenes „Verhalten" entwickeln und mit uns in einen „Dialog" treten können? An dieser Stelle erscheint es uns sinnvoll, die Begrifflichkeiten noch einmal etwas genauer zu beleuchten.

Fun Palace and Inter Action Centre, the visionary projects of the interaction-pioneer Cedric Price, were in the first instance nothing more than "skeletons"—the structurally necessary basic frameworks that would make further development simple, and would then have to be filled out with "content." The determining principle for Price was the idea that a building should come into being only through interaction with the people who wanted to use it, and should then continually change and adapt to new requirements of use. Where architecture and new technologies meet, one often hears such catchwords as "interactive spaces," "intelligent architectures," or "responsive environments". But what conceptions exactly are behind these ideas? What kind of interaction takes place between us and the architectures and objects described as "intelligent"? Does this mean that buildings will in future develop their own "behavior" and be able to engage in a "dialogue" with us? We think it meaningful at this point to examine these concepts again more precisely.

Usman Haque, dessen Projekte im Folgenden ausführlich vorgestellt werden, erforscht sehr präzise die Bedeutung der verschiedenen Konzepte. Stark beeinflusst wurde er nicht nur von den Ideen von Cedric Price, sondern auch von dem Kybernetiker Gordon Pask, der in den sechziger Jahren ebenfalls am Fun Palace mitarbeitete. Interaktivität ist dabei für Haque nicht zwingend an hochtechnisierte Anwendungen geknüpft:

„Interaktiv" und „hi-tech" sind keine untereinander austauschbaren Begriffe; man kann etwas schaffen, das interaktiv ist, aber keineswegs hi-tech (…) [und vice versa]. Durch technologische Fortschritte werden jedoch bestimmte Aspekte von Interaktivität leichter umsetzbar (…).[1]

In einem Interview mit plan a beschreibt Haque die unterschiedliche Bedeutung von „reaktiven", „interaktiven" und „lernenden" Systemen wie folgt:

Vieles, was sich „interaktiv" nennt, sind tatsächlich „reaktive" Architekturen und die Umsetzung „intelligenter" Architekturen ist so weit weg – ich denke, wir sollten uns zunächst einmal mit dem Bedeutung von Interaktivität auseinandersetzen. Nur weil bestimmte Arbeiten mit Begriffen wie „interaktiv" oder „intelligent" etikettiert wurden, bedeutet das noch lange nicht, dass wir dieses Ziel wirklich erreicht haben. (…)

Es besteht ein großer Unterschied zwischen den verschiedenen Ansätzen. Bei „reaktiven" Systemen ist das, was ich als

Usman Haque, whose projects are laid out in detail in what follows, investigates the meaning of the various concepts in a very precise way. He was strongly influenced not only by the ideas of Cedric Price, but also by the computer theorist Gordon Pask, who also worked on Fun Palace in the 1960s. Interactivity for Haque is not necessarily connected to highly technical applications:

"Interactive" and "hi-tech" are not interchangeable words; one can create something interactive yet not hi-tech … [and vice versa]. Technological advances may, however, make certain aspects of interaction easier to achieve.[1]…

In an interview with plan a, Haque explains the different meanings of "reactive," "interactive" and "learning" systems as follows:

Much of what calls itself "interactive" is actually "reactive" architecture and the implementation of "intelligent" architecture is so far off that we should deal with the interactive first. Just because some work has been labelled with the concept "interactive" or "intelligent" doesn't mean that we have actually achieved that goal. …

There is a big difference between the different approaches. In a reactive system what I call the "transfer function" is predetermined. So given a particular input you have a particular output. A simple example: you flip the switch and the light turns on. …

„Übertragungsfunktion" (transfer function) bezeichne, unveränderlich. Das heißt, Input und Output sind fix aneinander gekoppelt. Ein einfaches Beispiel: Du legst einen Schalter um und das Licht geht an. (…)

Die Mehrheit der vorgeblich „interaktiven Architekturen" basieren auf einer fixen Übertragungsfunktion: die Fassade, die ihre Farbe entsprechend der Umgebungstemperatur ändert oder das nette „Kunstwerk" im Empfangsbereich, das auf die vorbeilaufenden Menschen reagiert.[2]

Als „interaktiv" bezeichnet Haque dagegen solche Systeme, deren „Übertragungsfunktion" veränderlich ist. Dieser Fall tritt etwa ein, wenn es mehrere Möglichkeiten gibt, Input und Output miteinander zu verknüpfen.[3] Haque erläutert das am einfachen Beispiel eines Thermostats:

Ein Thermostat funktioniert normalerweise so, dass die Umgebungstemperatur [Input] gemessen und abhängig von der gewünschten Raumtemperatur dann die Heizung entweder herauf- oder heruntergefahren wird [Output]. Die Transferfunktion ist in gewissem Sinne variabel, weil sie sowohl die Umgebung als die Einstellung bewertet, die die gewünschte Temperatur setzt. Andererseits ist sie fix, denn sie misst nur die Temperatur und kontrolliert immer nur die Heizung. Wie wird das Thermostat nun zu einem interaktiven System? Ein erster Schritt wäre es, wenn verschiedene Eingangsdaten zur Verfügung stehen würden – das könnte zum Beispiel die Temperatur im Außenraum, mein Energieverbrauch im letzten Monat oder auch die Anzahl der Menschen im

But most of the so called "interactive architecture" is based on this fixed transfer function: the façade that changes color with temperature, or the piece of lobby art that responds to people walking through.[2]

Haque describes as "interactive" those systems, where the "transfer function" is variable. This is the case for example when there are multiple possibilities for connecting input and output.[3] Haque explains this using the simple example of a thermostat:

The usual way a thermostat functions is that the surrounding temperature [input] is measured and then on the basis of the desired room temperature the heating is turned up or down [output]. The transfer function is in some senses variable, because it is constantly evaluating both the environment and the dial that sets the desired temperature, but can also be viewed as fixed, because it is always measuring only temperature and is always controlling only a heater. How could the thermostat be made into a real interactive system? The first step would be if there were a range of types of input—the weather outside, my energy use in the last month or the number of people in the room—and there would also be a whole set of outputs, like turning on the heating, closing the window, or keeping my energy use as low as possible. …

What kinds of input produce what kinds of output can be determined by events outside of the system of rules, for example by the inf-luence of the person. It is a further step when a system has been developed that is

Raum sein – und diese eine Vielzahl möglicher Ausgabegrößen bewirken würden, wie die Aufforderung, die Heizung einzuschalten, die Fenster zu schließen oder meinen Energie-verbrauch möglichst gering zu halten. (…)

Welche Eingangsdaten welche Art von Ergebnis herbeiführen, kann dabei durch ein Ereignis außerhalb des Regelkreislaufes – zum Beispiel durch die Einflussnahme des Menschen – bestimmt werden. (…)

Noch eine Stufe weiter ist ein System dann entwickelt, wenn es fähig ist zu lernen – das heißt, wenn es seine Eigenschaften aufgrund seiner Interaktion mit seiner Außenwelt selb-ständig modifizieren und sich so anpassen kann. (…)[4]

Diese Überlegungen verdeutlichen, dass „interaktive Architekturen" nicht gleichzusetzen sind mit Räumen, die mit sämtlichen tech-nischen Geräten „aufgerüstet" sind, uns jeden Handgriff abnehmen und unseren Alltag automatisieren, sondern dass es hier vielmehr darum geht, Möglichkeiten der Partizipation zu schaffen. Offensichtlich wird auch, wie groß der Unterschied zwischen bloßer Reaktion und einer komplexen, intelligenten Konversation ist, die auf der beidseitigen Fähigkeit des Ver-stehens gründet. Doch welche Potentiale für die Architektur sind mit dem Konzept von Inter-aktivität verbunden? Usman Haque bemerkt dazu:

Mich beschäftigt sehr stark, dass der einzelne Mensch in einem Gebäude und in der Stadt immer weniger wichtig ist. Wir geben

capable of learning—this means, when it can itself modify its own qualities on the basis of its interaction with its environment and thus adjust to it. …[4]

These considerations make it clear that "interactive architectures" are not simply spaces that are "equipped" with all of the possible technical devices for relieving us of having to carry out various actions and automating our everyday life; here it is rather about creating possibilities for participation. It also becomes clear how great the difference is between mere reaction and a complex conversation based on a capacity for under-standing on both sides. But what potential is there for architecture in the concept of interactivity? Usman Haque observes here:

What concerns me is that the individual person becomes less and less important in building or in the city. We hand over the whole responsibility to companies or architects. We walk around through our cities feeling that we have not made them or had a say in how they are made. We are reduced to mere bystanders, mere "users." …

All of these "intelligent houses" spread the myth that one has to use particular systems, for example Microsoft, in order to use new technologies. I disagree with this. That is why Adam [Somlai-Fischer] and I developed the Reconfigurable House (see p. 26) We used cheap toys and gadgets that really non-technical people can hack, and based the installation on open source-software. Anyone who wanted to could participate. …

die ganze Verantwortung ab an Unternehmen oder auch an Architekten. Wir laufen durch unsere Städte mit dem Gefühl, sie nicht selber geschaffen, nicht mitbestimmt zu haben. Wir werden zu Statisten, zu bloßen „Nutzern" degradiert. (…)

All diese „intelligenten Häuser" verbreiten das Märchen, dass man auf bestimmte Systeme, zum Beispiel auf Microsoft angewiesen ist, um neue Technologien nutzen zu können. Dem stimme ich absolut nicht zu. Das war auch der Grund, warum Adam [Somlai-Fischer] und ich Reconfigurable House (siehe S. 22) entwickelt haben. Wir haben billiges Elektronikspielzeug verwendet, das auch Leute ohne Programmierkenntnisse einfach hacken können, und die Installation basierend auf Open-Source-Software aufgebaut. Jeder, der wollte, konnte daran teilnehmen. (…)

Der eben skizzierte Ansatz von „Interaktivität" ermöglicht uns, die traditionelle Trennung in der Architektur zwischen Hersteller und Verbraucher – zwischen Designer, Eigentümer und „Nutzer" – in Frage zu stellen. Es geht darum, Instrumente zu entwickeln, mit denen die Menschen selber ihre Umwelt gestalten und mehr Verantwortung übernehmen können. (…)

Bei meinem Projekt Burble (siehe S. 124) kamen zum Beispiel ganz „normale" Menschen zusammen, um eine Installation von der Größe eines fünfzehnstöckigen Hochhauses selbst zusammenzubauen und für einen Abend in den Himmel aufsteigen zu lassen. Einer der schönsten Momente war für

This approach to "interactivity" allows us to challenge the traditional division in architecture between designer, client, and "user". It is about designing tools that people themselves may use to construct (in the widest sense) their environments and take on more responsibility. …

With my project Burble (see p. 124), members of the public came together to assemble a structure on the scale a fifteen-storey building and let it up into the sky. One of the most gratifying things in the project came afterwards when somebody wrote in a blog how proud they were of to have achieved that. …

Of course I am aware that not everyone wants to configure their own environment all of the time, rather that participation is bound up with various motivations and capacities. What interests me is the granularity of the way people could participate. You don't have to understand computer software down to the smallest detail in order to create your own applications. … This was our approach with Pachube (see p. 138). It is a webservice for connecting up real and virtual spaces around the world, based on a very simple programming language. People can then develop their own individual applications and add different inputs and outputs. This is where the interaction comes about.[5]

mich, als im Anschluss jemand in einen Blog schrieb, wie stolz er darauf war, das geschafft zu haben. (…)

Natürlich ist mir bewusst, dass nicht jeder jederzeit sein Umfeld selber gestalten möchte, sondern Partizipiation immer mit unterschiedlichen Motivationen und Fähigkeiten verbunden ist. Mich interessiert es daher sehr, verschiedene Ebenen der Partizipation zu ermöglichen. Man muss eine Computersoftware nicht bis ins letzte Detail verstehen, um selbst Anwendungen entwickeln zu können. (…) Diesen Ansatz verfolgen wir auch mit Pachube (siehe S. 138). Der Webservice, mit dem reale und virtuelle Räume weltweit miteinander verbunden werden können, basiert auf einer sehr einfachen Programmiersprache. Die Menschen können dann eigenständig ihre individuellen Anwendungen entwickeln und verschiedene Inputs und Outputs hinzufügen. Hier entsteht für mich Interaktion.[5]

1 Auszug aus dem Thesenpapier / Excerpt from the thesis paper: Usman Haque: Architecture, interaction, systems, 2006

2 Interview Usman Haque mit / with plan a, 11.12.2008

3 Vgl. / see: Hugh Dubberly / Usman Haque / Paul Pangaro: What is interaction? Are there different types?, interactions, XVI.1, Jan./Feb. 2009

4 Interview Usman Haque mit / with plan a, 11.12.2008

5 ebenda / ibid.

19
Open Burble

Open Burble / Haque Design + Research (UK) / 2006

Premiere feierte Open Burble anlässlich der
Biennale in Singapur im Jahr 2006.
2007 wurde die Installation auch im Londoner
Holland Park aufgeführt.
Open Burble celebrated its premiere at the 2006
Biennale in Singapore. In 2007 the installation
was presented in London's Holland Park.

Burble ist ein imposantes Gefüge aus ca.
1000 Heliumballons, die durch ein Gitter aus
Carbonfaserstäben zusammengehalten werden.
In jeden Ballon sind Sensoren, Mikrokontroller
und LEDs integriert, die Burble in ein buntes
Lichtermeer verwandeln. Das Publikum – hier
Zuschauer und Ausführende zugleich – baut
Burble nicht nur selbst zusammen, sondern
muss anschließend auch die Kontrolle über die
Installation behalten: Fertig montiert, steigt
Burble hinauf in den Abendhimmel, wird vom
Wind durcheinandergewirbelt und leuchtet in
zahlreichen Farben. Allein durch das Gewicht
der versammelten Menschen, die an einem
langen, mit Sensoren ausgestatteten Griff am
unteren Ende der Struktur festhalten, wird
Burble am Davonfliegen gehindert. Das Publikum kann Burble so immer wieder neu
ausrichten – gleichzeitig resultieren die Bewegungen der Menschen in einem Farbecho, das
sich über die gesamte Struktur verteilt. Via
Infrarotschnittstellen kommunizieren die Heliumballons miteinander, sodass zusammenhängende
Farbmuster entstehen. Mit Burble – die Installation ist so hoch wie ein fünfzehnstöckiges
Gebäude – erobern die Menschen den Stadtraum, wenn auch nur für einen Abend.

Burble is an imposing structure of
around 1000 helium balloons, held together
by a lattice of carbon fiber rods. Sensors,
micro-controllers, and LEDs are integrated
into each balloon, transforming Burble into a
colorful sea of light. The public—here spectators and performers at the same time—
don't just put Burble together, but must also
then maintain control over the installation:
once assembled, Burble floats up into the
evening sky, is whirled about by the wind,
and lights up in a multitude of colors. Only
the weight of the assembled people, hanging
on to a long, sensor-equipped handle at the
bottom end of the structure, stop Burble
from flying away. The spectators can align
Burble in many new ways, and at the same
time their movements result in a color echo,
dispersed across the entire structure. The
helium balloons communicate with each
other by way of infrared interfaces, such that
coherent color patterns arise. With Burble—
the installation is as high as a five-story
building—the people conquer the city space,
if only for an evening.

20
Behaving Architecture

Slow Furl / Mette Ramsgard Thomsen, Karin Bech (CITA / DK) / 2008
Vivisection / Mette Ramsgard Thomsen (CITA / DK), Simon Lovind
(Danmark Design Skole / DK) / 2006

limited

control

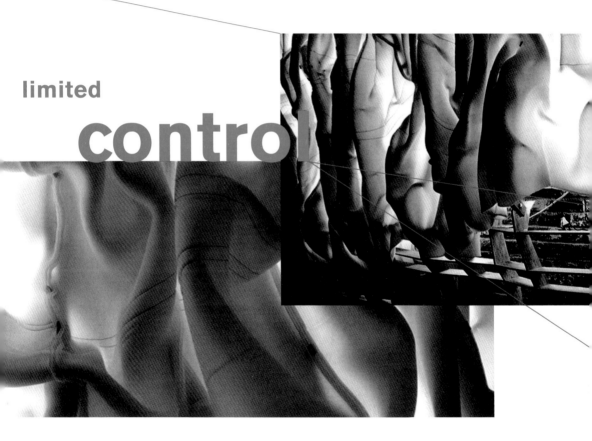

Behaving Architecture – eine Architektur, die ein eigenes Verhalten entwickelt – erforscht die dänische Wissenschaftlerin und Architektin Mette Ramsgard Thomsen mit ihren Kollegen am Center for Information Technology and Architecture (CITA) an der Kunstakademie Kopenhagen. Sie versteht unsere gebaute Umwelt als einen dynamischen Ort des Austauschs und der Kommunikation und ihre Arbeiten untersuchen, wie Architektur als responsives System gedacht, entworfen und realisiert werden kann, das das „Verhalten" seiner Wände, Fußböden und Decken zu den Veränderungen in seiner äußeren, aber auch inneren Umgebung in Beziehung setzt. Was das konkret heißt, zeigen die Installationen Slow Furl und Vivisection.

Slow Furl ist eine raumgreifende Textilinstallation, die im Juni 2008 in der Lighthouse Gallery in Brighton ausgestellt wurde. Der gesamte Raum wird von einer elastischen Oberfläche, einer Robotermembran, umschlossen. Besucher können diese berühren oder inmitten der weichen Wände sitzen. Wie eine Landschaft oder eine Wolkenformation verändert sich das Textil langsam und formt sich um den Körper des Benutzers. Anstatt jedoch Bewegungen im Raum einfach nur „abzubilden", definiert Slow Furl seine eigene Zeitlichkeit jenseits der sofortigen Reaktion.

Behaving Architecture—an architecture that develops its own behavior—is being investigated by the Danish scientist and architect Mette Ramsgard Thomsen with her colleagues at the Center for Information Technology and Architecture (CITA) at the Royal Danish Academy of Fine Arts in Copenhagen. She understands our built environment as a dynamic space of exchange and communication, and her work investigates how architecture can be thought, designed, and realized as a responsive system that can relate the "behavior" of its walls, floors, and ceilings both to changes outside and also to its internal environment. What this means concretely is shown by the installations Slow Furl and Vivisection.

Slow Furl a space-encompassing textile installation, exhibited in June 2008 at the Lighthouse Gallery in Brighton. The entire space is enclosed in an elastic surface, a robot-membrane. Visitors can touch it, or sit amidst the soft walls. Like a landscape or a cloud formation, the fabric changes slowly and forms itself around the body of the user. Rather than merely "mirroring" movements in the space however, Slow Furl defines its own sense of time beyond immediate reaction.

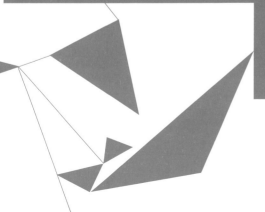

Unter der textilen Oberfläche von Slow Furl befindet sich eine Tragstruktur, deren mechanische Bewegung durch Mikrocomputer aktiviert und gesteuert wird. Diese Bewegungen laufen einerseits nach einem programmierten Zyklus ab. Gleichzeitig werden sie aber auch durch die Besucher beeinflusst, da die gesamte Oberfläche von Slow Furl mit berührungssensiblen Sensoren versehen ist. Der Wechsel zwischen Selbstaktivierung durch die programmierten Bewegungszyklen und Reaktion auf Berührung und Bewegung der Menschen im Raum verleiht Slow Furl eine inhärente Unbestimmtheit. Architektur „verhält sich" hier eher, als dass sie interagiert.

Under the textile surface of Slow Furl is a supporting structure whose mechanical movements are activated and controlled by microcomputers. These movements are on the one hand executed in accordance with a programmed cycle. At the same time, however, they are influenced by the visitors, since the entire surface of Slow Furl is fitted with touch-sensitive sensors. The alternation between self-activation by the programmed movement cycles and reaction to the touch and movement of people in the space gives Slow Furl an inherent indeterminacy. Architecture "behaves itself" here more than it interacts.

Auch **Vivisection** basiert auf der Idee einer sensiblen Oberfläche, die die Anwesenheit von Besuchern „spürt" – einer Haut, die agiert und auf ihre Benutzung reagiert. Während Slow Furl sich langsam und fast schwerfällig in seiner eigenen Geschwindigkeit bewegt, erscheint Vivisection leichter, agiler, fast schwebend. In das Seide-Stahl-Gewebe sind zusätzlich Sensoren integriert, die mit einem Netzwerk von Mikrocomputern verbunden sind. Dadurch werden Gebläse gesteuert, die in das Textil eingewobene Hohlräume mit Luft füllen oder ihnen diese entziehen. Der Stoff „atmet", „pulsiert", „antwortet" auf die Gegenwart der Besucher. Vivisection ist ein „Sensing Space" im wahrsten Sinne des Wortes: Die Oberfläche selbst wird zum wahrnehmenden Subjekt.

Vivisection is also based on the idea of a sensitive surface, which "senses" the presence of visitors—a skin that acts and reacts to being used. While Slow Furl moves slowly and almost ponderously at its own speed, Vivisection seems lighter, more agile, almost levitating. Extra sensors are integrated into the silk-steel texture and connected to a network of microcomputers. These control fans that pump air into or out of hollows woven into the textile. The fabric "breathes," "pulsates," and "answers" to the presence of the visitors. Vivisection is a "sensing space" in the truest sense of the word: the surface itself becomes a perceiving subject.

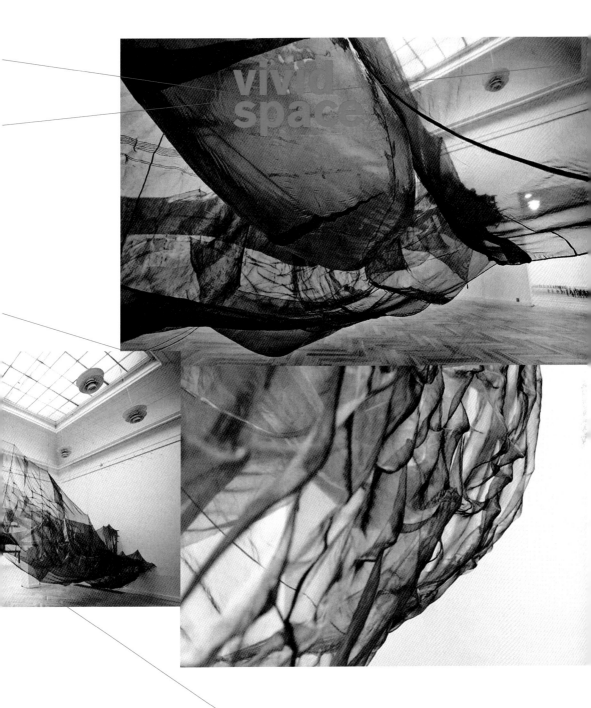

vivid
space

131

21

Learning Architecture?

Performative Ecologies / Ruairi Glynn (UK) / 2008
Angels – Constructing Reconfigurable Space / Ruairi Glynn,
Paul Burres (UK) / 2006

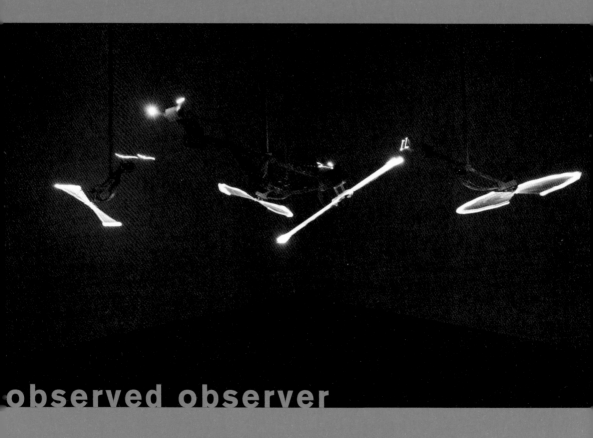

observed observer

Der britische Architekt Ruairi Glynn beschäftigt sich seit einigen Jahren intensiv mit Konzepten für interaktive Architekturen. Zum einen stellt er auf seinem Onlineportal interactivearchitecture.org Projekte von Architekten, Künstlern, Designern und Wissenschaftlern vor, die weltweit an diesem Thema arbeiten. Zum anderen untersucht er in eigenen architektonischen Experimenten und Prototypen Potenziale eines tatsächlich interaktiven Raumes, der nicht nur auf seine Umgebung reagiert, sondern mit ihr in einen Dialog tritt.

Bei **Performative Ecologies** beispielsweise wird der Beobachter zum Beobachteten: Die „tanzenden" Roboter registrieren den Grad der Aufmerksamkeit, den sie für ihr Performance erhalten und richten ihr Verhalten dementsprechend aus. Die preisgekrönte Installation ist ein kinetisches „Konversationsumfeld" – ein Raum, der sich durch die Interaktion zwischen Mensch und Technologie beständig verändert. Der Tanz der Roboter ist nicht vorchoreografiert, vielmehr wird er im Dialog mit dem Publikum entwickelt – die Roboter „lernen", wie sie am besten Aufmerksamkeit erregen und erhalten. Über Gesichtserkennungssoftware registrieren sie, ob die Betrachter ihre Bewegungen verfolgen – ob also gefällt, was sie tun. Dabei bleibt letztendlich offen, wer auf wen reagiert. Beeinflusst die Maschine den Menschen oder der Mensch die Maschine?

For some years, the British architect Ruairi Glynn has been intensively thinking through ideas for an interactive architecture. On the one hand, his online portal, interactivearchitecture.org, presents projects by architects, artists, designers and scientists working on this subject around the world. On the other hand, he uses his own architectural experiments and prototypes to investigate the potential of a genuinely interactive space, one that not only reacts to its surroundings, but also engages in dialogue with it.

In **Performative Ecologies**, for example, the observer becomes the observed: the "dancing" robots register the degree of attention they get for their performance, and direct their behavior accordingly. This prize-winning installation is a kinetic "conversation-area"—a space that constantly changes through the interaction of human and technology. The dance of the robots is not prechoreographed, but rather developed in dialogue with the audience—the robots "learn," how best to excite and then maintain attention. Using face-recognition software, they register whether observers follow their movements—whether people like what they do. It is an open question though, who is reacting to whom. Does the machine influence the person or the person the machine?

Jede der vier robotischen Skulpturen besteht aus einer Plexiglas-Stahl-Aluminium-Konstruktion, ihre Bewegungen werden über Servomotoren gesteuert. Integrierte RGB-Leuchten ermöglichen es den Robotern, in ihrer Lichtperformance das volle Farbenspektrum zu nutzen. Außerdem können sie sich komplett um die eigene Achse bewegen. Ihre Aktionen werden aus einem auf genetischen Algorithmen (G.A.) basierenden Pool generiert, der auf Gesichtserkennungssoftware zurückgreift, um die Performance entsprechend zu variieren. Sind keine Menschen im Raum, performen die Roboter füreinander und stimmen ihre Bewegungen aufeinander ab. Performative Ecologies wurde unter anderem im Foyer des Kunsthauses Graz gezeigt, wo die Roboter sogar lernten, auf vorbeigehende Passanten zu reagieren und sie fast in den Ausstellungsraum hereinwinkten – ein im wahrsten Sinne des Wortes einladender Raum.

Each of the four robotic sculptures consists of a plexiglas-steel-aluminum construction; their movements are controlled by servomotors. Integrated RGB-lights make it possible for the robots to use the full color spectrum in their light performances. They can also move completely around their own axis. Their actions are generated from a pool based on genetic algorithms, referring back to face-recognition software, in order to vary the performance accordingly. If there are no humans in the room, the robots perform just for themselves, and coordinate their movements with each other. Performative Ecologies has been shown, among other places, in the Foyer of the Kunst-haus Graz, where the robots learned to react to passing pedestrians, almost beckoning them into the exhibition hall—an inviting space in the truest sense of the word.

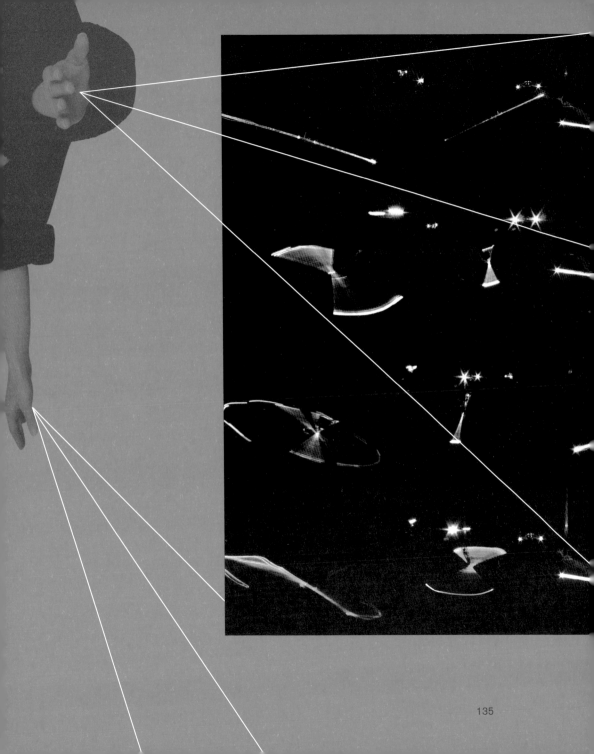

Ist es möglich, Architekturen zu entwickeln, die auf das Verhalten der Personen im Raum reagieren und sich physisch verändern? Glynn erforscht diese Idee auch mit seinem **Angel**-Projekt. Einen ersten Prototypen hat er mit seinem Partner Paul Burres an der Bartlett School of Architecture bereits gebaut: ein mit Helium gefüllter „Testballon", der auf Gesten, Nähe und Gespräche der Personen im Raum reagiert, entsprechend seine Position verändert und dadurch wiederum Einfluss auf das Verhalten der Menschen in seiner Umgebung nimmt. Eine Kamera und Sensoren an Bord des Angel übermittelten Daten aus dem Raum zu einem Computer, der mit Hilfe einer Software eine sich analog zu den Daten verändernde Projektion an einer Wand des Raumes generierte. Dadurch wurde den Besuchern ein zusätzliches Feedback zu ihren Aktionen geboten. Während der erste Angel-Prototyp nur „reagierte", ist bei zukünftigen Versionen denkbar, dass der Angel, ähnlich wie Performative Ecologies, sich den Verhaltensweisen seiner Umgebung anpasst und fähig ist, zu „lernen". Glynns Forschungsinteresse ist dabei geleitet von Fragen wie: Inwieweit können Maschinen ein „Verständnis" für solche komplexen Vorgänge wie menschliche Konversation erlangen?

Is it possible to develop architectures that change physically in reaction to the behavior of people in space? Glynn investigates this idea with his **Angel**-project. He has already built a first prototype with his partner Paul Burres at the Bartlett School of Architecture: a helium-filled "test balloon" that reacts to the gestures, proximity, and conversations of people in the room, changes its position correspondingly, and thereby exerts an influence on the behavior of people in its vicinity. A camera and sensors on board the Angel relayed data from the room to a computer, which used software to generate a projection on the wall of the room which changed in response to the incoming data. This provided the visitors with additional feedback on their actions. While the first Angel-prototype merely "reacted," it is conceivable that future versions of the Angel will, as was the case with Performative Ecologies, adapt to the behavior patterns of their surroundings and be capable of "learning." Glynn's research interest is guided here by such questions as: to what extent can machines attain an "understanding" of such complex processes as human conversation?

22
Responsive Environments

Pachube / Haque Design + Research (UK) / seit / since 2007
Natural Fuse / Haque Design + Research (UK) / seit / since 2008

Einfach formuliert, handelt es sich bei **Pachube** um einen Webservice – ein bisschen wie YouTube – nur dass hier keine Videos untereinander ausgetauscht werden, sondern via Internet weltweit und in Echtzeit die Daten von Sensoren. Mittels Pachube können so reale wie auch virtuelle Einzelgeräte, Objekte und komplexe Räume – zum Beispiel Laptops, Mobiltelefone, ganze Gebäude, aber auch Webpages oder interaktive Installationen – verbunden werden und miteinander „kommunizieren". Die Vision, die hinter diesem Konzept von dynamisch in Austausch tretenden „Umgebungen" steckt, ist eng mit dem Ansatz vom „Internet der Dinge" verbunden: In Zukunft werden immer mehr unserer Alltagsgegenstände elektronisch vernetzt sein und sich in ständigem Informationsaustausch

Simply formulated, **Pachube** is a Webservice. It is a little bit like YouTube, except that here no videos are exchanged, but rather the data of sensors, in real time over the internet. Using Pachube, real and also virtual stand-alone devices, objects, and complex spaces—for example laptops, mobile phones, whole buildings, but also webpages or interactive installations— can be connected and communicate with each other. The vision behind this idea of bringing "settings" into dynamic exchange is closely connected with the concept of an "internet of things": in the future, more and more of our everyday objects will be electronically networked and will be in

miteinander befinden, um uns bei unseren Tätigkeiten zu unterstützen. Das Internet, so die Annahme, wird sich mit mobilen Anwendungen über seine klassische Domäne hinaus ausbreiten. In dieser extremen Vernetzung stecken unzählige, noch zu erforschende Potenziale für neue Dienstleistungen und Produkte. Diese Möglichkeiten nicht allein einigen wenigen Unternehmen zu überlassen, bildet ein essenzielles Anliegen der Entwickler von Pachube. In Anlehnung an den „Open-Source-Gedanken" soll jeder – auch wenn er kein Technikexperte oder Softwareentwickler ist – an den Potenzialen des Internets teilhaben können.

constant information exchange with one other, in order to support us in our activities. Mobile applications will, on this assumption, spread the internet beyond its classical domains. This extreme networking contains innumerable unexplored potential opportunities for new services and products. A fundamental intention of the Pachube developers was that these possibilities not just be left to a few companies. Following the "Open-Source Idea," the idea is that everyone—even if they are not technical experts or software developers—should be able to participate in the potential of the internet.

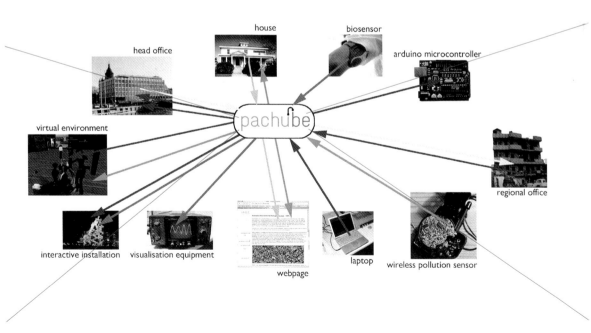

head office
house
biosensor
arduino microcontroller
pachube
virtual environment
regional office
interactive installation
visualisation equipment
webpage
laptop
wireless pollution sensor

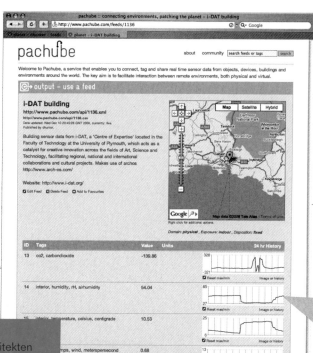

Der Webservice soll zukünftig Architekten und Designer unterstützen – einerseits bei der Entwicklung ihrer Gebäude, indem in Echtzeit grundstücksspezifische Daten zur Verfügung gestellt werden, weiterhin auch bei der Optimierung der anschließenden Gebäudenutzung. Nach Haque werden sich Gebäude in Zukunft in ständigem Informationsaustausch miteinander befinden, über Energieverbrauch, Ressourcenmanagement, Auslastungsgrad etc., und sogar von den Strategien der anderen „lernen" können (siehe Beitrag, S. 119).

In future the web service should support achitects and designers in the development of their buildings, by providing building-site-specific data in real time, and beyond this also in the optimization of the eventual building use. According to Haque, buildings will in future be in continual information exchange with one another, regarding energy use, resource management, degree of utilization, etc., and buildings will even be able to "learn" from the strategies of other buildings (see text, p. 119).

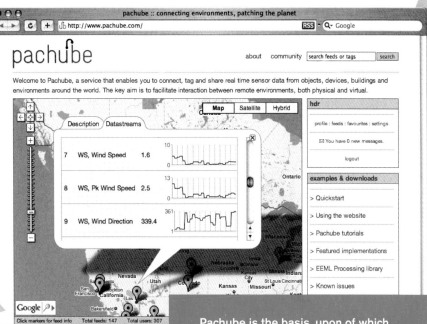

Pachube bildet die Basis, von der aus spezifische Anwendungen entwickelt werden können. Bereits heute wird Pachube genutzt, um zum Beispiel den Energieverbrauch eines Gebäudes via PDA oder Laptop in Echtzeit zu überwachen und gegebenenfalls steuernd einzugreifen. Auch für das Projekt Scattered House (siehe S. 30) fand Pachube Anwendung und vernetzte das „Haus" in London mit weiteren Orten weltweit. Eine andere Anwendung ist das Projekt Natural Fuse (siehe S. 142).

Pachube is the basis, upon of which specific applications can be developed. Pachube is already being used, for example, to monitor the energy use of a building via PDA or laptop in real time, and if necessary to take corrective action. Pachube was also used for the project Scattered House (see p. 30) to network the London "house" with further locations worldwide. Another application was the project Natural Fuse (see p. 142).

141

Mit kleinen elektronischen Bauteilen ausge-
stattete und untereinander vernetzte Pflanzen
werden zu einer „natürlichen Sicherung"
(natural fuse), die den Stromfluss unterbrechen,
sobald zu viel Energie verbraucht wird.
Fitted out with tiny electronic components and
networked together, the plants become a
natural fuse, which interrupts the power supply
as soon as too much energy is used.

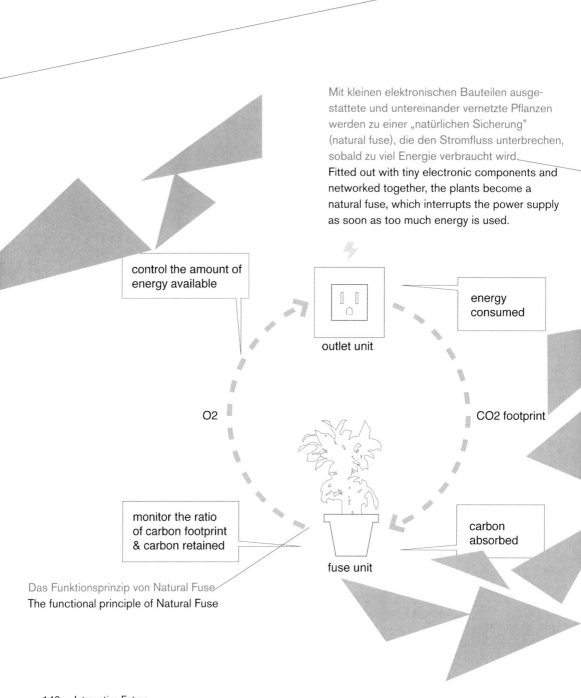

control the amount of
energy available

outlet unit

energy
consumed

O2

CO2 footprint

monitor the ratio
of carbon footprint
& carbon retained

carbon
absorbed

fuse unit

Das Funktionsprinzip von Natural Fuse
The functional principle of Natural Fuse

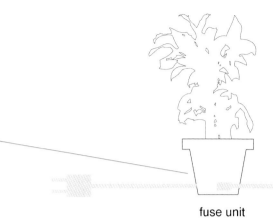

fuse unit

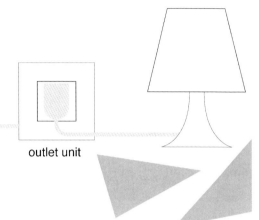

outlet unit

Natural Fuse ist ein „natürlicher Schutz-
schalter", der einem zu hohen Energieverbrauch
in Haushalten und damit einer unausgeglichenen
CO_2-Bilanz entgegenwirken soll. Das Projekt
basiert auf einem stadtweiten System von
untereinander vernetzten und mit kleinen, elektronischen Bauteilen ausgestatteten Pflanzen,
deren Eigenschaft, als CO_2-Senke zu fungieren,
hier genutzt wird. Das Ziel ist es, innerhalb
dieses Systems nur so viel CO_2 durch die
Haushalte (zum Beispiel durch elektronische
Geräte) freizusetzen, wie durch die Pflanzen
kompensiert werden kann. Wird das System im
Gleichgewicht gehalten, blühen und gedeihen
die Pflanzen: Ihre Wasserversorgung wird elektronisch reguliert, was jedoch nur so lange
funktioniert, wie genügend Energie für diese
Steuerung „übrig" bleibt.

Natural Fuse is intended to work
against excessive household energy use,
and thereby reduce carbon emissions. The
project is based on a citywide system of
networked plants, fitted with tiny electronic
components, and whose ability to act as
carbon sinks is here put to use. The aim
is that only as much CO_2 should be produced by the households within the system (e.g., with electronic devices), as can
be compensated for by the plants. If the
system is kept in balance, the plants thrive
and blossom: their water supply is electronically regulated, and functions only as
long as there is enough energy "left over"
to control it.

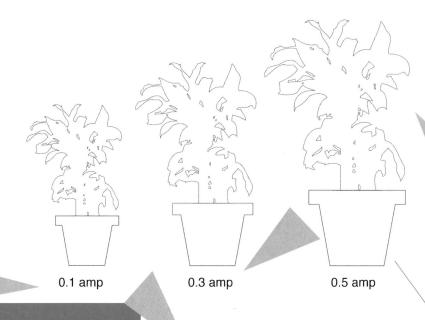

0.1 amp   0.3 amp   0.5 amp

Ist die CO$_2$-Bilanz negativ, fällt die Wasser-versorgung aus, die Pflanzen sterben, der Stromfluss wird damit unterbrochen und gleich-zeitig auch die Energiekapazität im gesamten System reduziert. Der Informationsaustausch der Pflanzen untereinander wird durch den Webservice Pachube gewährleistet (siehe S. 138). Natural Fuse wurde ermöglicht durch die Unterstützung der „Architectural League" in New York, im Rahmen der Ausstellung „Situated Technologies: Toward the Sentient City." Geplant ist, die ersten vernetzten Pflanzen im Herbst 2009 an New Yorker Haushalte auszuteilen.

If the CO$_2$ balance is negative, the water supply is cut off, the plants die, the electricity supply is interrupted and the energy capa-city of the whole system is thereby reduced. The information exchange of the plants with each other is provided for by the web service Pachube (see p. 138). Natural Fuse was made possible by the support of the Architectural League in New York, as part of the Exhibition "Situated Technologies: Toward the Sentient City." The plan is to distribute the first networked plants to New York households in the Fall of 2009.

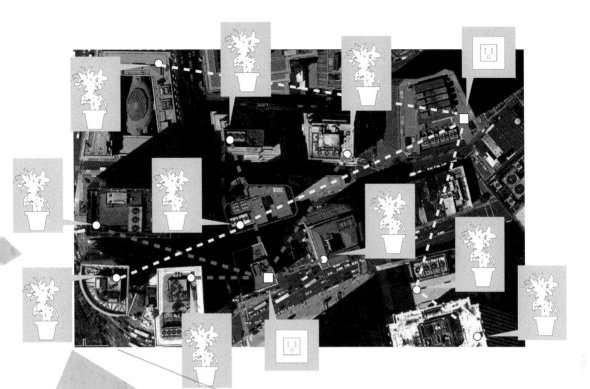

Die CO₂-Bilanz ist „direkt ablesbar" am Wohlergehen der Pflanzen. Ihre Wasserversorgung funktioniert nur, wenn genügend Energie innerhalb des Systems „übrig" ist.

The CO_2-Balance is "directly readable" from the welfare of the plants. Their water supply only functions when enough energy is "left over" in the system.

Damit der Strom nicht ausfällt, müssen die Leute kooperieren, denn der Energieverbrauch wird innerhalb aller im Netzwerk integrierten Haushalte reguliert.

In order that their electricity not be cut off, participants must cooperate with one another, since energy use is regulated between all of the households integrated into the network.

Fast Forward

Forschungsfeld Interaktive Architekturen
Research Field Interactive Architecture

Gebäude als Teil eines komplexen „Öko-systems" aus miteinander vernetzten Geräten, Sensoren, Bauwerken und virtuellen Räumen. Häuser, die untereinander kommunizieren und Informationen über ihren Energieverbrauch, ihre Belegungsrate und notwendige Wartungs-arbeiten austauschen und sogar voneinander „lernen". Räume, die nicht nur auf unsere Präsenz reagieren, sondern die wir selber mit-gestalten und uns so aneignen können; die vielleicht sogar ein eigenes, immer wieder modifiziertes Verhalten zeigen und fähig sind, sich selbst „weiterzuentwickeln". Weltweit wird an der Zukunft interaktiver Räume geforscht und experimentiert, einen Einblick geben die auf den vorangegangenen Seiten beschrie-benen Ansätze. Für eine weiterführende Recherche haben wir im Folgenden Links zu-sammengestellt, die über die Projektauswahl von „Sensing Space" hinaus aktuelle Informa-tionen zur Entwicklung im Bereich Architektur und Technologie, insbesondere zu Experi-menten, Prototypen und Untersuchungen im Feld der Interaktivität von Architektur und Design liefern.

A building as part of a complex "ecosystem" of networked devices, sensors, building complexes, and virtual spaces. Houses that communicate with one another, exchange information about their energy use, occupancy levels, and necessary maintenance and even "learn" from each other. Rooms that not only react to our presence, but which we can ourselves co-design and thus adapt to our needs; which perhaps are even capable of continuously producing new behaviors of their own and "further developing" themselves. The future of interactive space is the subject of research and experimentation worldwide, as shown by the approaches presented on the preceding pages. For further information, we have compiled the following links, which present up-to-date information on develop-ments in architecture and technology beyond the selection of "Sensing Space". The include, in particular, experiments, prototypes and investigations in the field of the interactivity of architecture and design.

Forschungsinstitutionen (Auswahl)
Research Institutions (selection)

Bartlett Interactive Architecture Workshop, UK:
www.bartlett.ucl.ac.uk/architecture/resources/i_workshop/i_workshop.htm

Die Forschungseinheit unter der Leitung von Stephen Gage an der Londoner Bartlett School of Architecture fokussiert auf die „ästhetischen und pragmatischen Möglichkeiten einer zu ihrer Umgebung responsiven Architektur". Im Rahmen des Workshops werden Arbeiten von aktuellen und ehemaligen Studenten unterstützt. So sind die hier vorgestellten Arbeiten Angels und Performative Ecologies (siehe S. 113) von Ruairi Glynn im Rahmen des Workshops entstanden.

The research group directed by Stephen Gage at the London Bartlett School of Architecture focuses on the "aesthetic and pragmatic possibilities of an architecture that responds to its environment." The workshop supports the work of current and former students. Two of the works presented here, Angels und Performative Ecologies (see p.113) by Ruairi Glynn, were created in the context of this workshop

Center for Information Technology and Architecture, DK:
http://cita.karch.dk/

Angesiedelt an der Königlichen Kunstakademie Kopenhagen, erforscht das Center for Information Technology and Architecture unter der Leitung von Mette Ramsgard Thomsen den Einfluss digitaler Kultur auf Theorie und Praxis in der Architektur. Neben dem Forschungsbereich „Behaving Architectures", in dem auch die vorgestellten Projekte Slow Furl und Vivisection (siehe S. 126) angesiedelt sind, arbeiten die Forscher am CITA zu den Themen „Digital Formations", insbesondere zum Einfluss von Rapid-Prototyping-Technologien auf die Architektur, und zu „Interface Ecologies", der Schnittstelle zwischen virtueller und physischer Umwelt.

Residing at the Royal Danish Academy of Fine Arts in Copenhagen, the Center for Information Technology and Architecture. under the direction of Mette Ramsgard Thomsen, investigates the influence of digital culture on the theory and practice of architecture. Beyond the research area "Behaving Architectures," which included the projects Slow Furl and Vivisection presented here (see p. 126), the researchers at CITA are working on the subjects of "Digital Formations," with emphasis on the influence of Rapid-Prototyping-Technologies on architecture, and of "Interface Ecologies," the interface between the virtual and physical environment.

House_n, Massachusetts Institute of Technology, USA
http://architecture.mit.edu/house_n

House_n ist eine Forschungsgruppe der Architekturabteilung des MIT, die untersucht, wie neue Technologien, Materialien und Designstrategien dynamische, sich verändernde

Räume schaffen können. Hauptinitiativen von House_n sind das PlaceLAb und die Open Source Building Alliance. House_n entwickelt unter anderem Technologien und Design-strategien, basierend auf „Context-Aware"-Sensoren, die Informationen über Entschei-dungsprozesse und Aktivitäten liefern. Die Forscher konzentrieren sich auf drei An-wendungsgebiete: Gesundheit („pro-aktive Umgebungen für eine gesunde Lebensweise"), Energie (Strategien für Nullenergiehäuser) und Massenanfertigung (Bauträgerkomponenten für Wohnräume). So arbeitet House_n unter anderem an physischen und digitalen Systemen, die zu Hause und im öffentlichen Raum einen gesunden Lebensstil fördern sollen. Es wurden zum Beispiel Technologien entwickelt und in Boston getestet, um Menschen zur Benutzung der Treppe statt eines Aufzugs zu motivieren.

House_n is a research group in the archi-tecture department of MIT, which investigates how new technologies, materials, and design strategies can create dynamic, self-altering spaces. The primary initiatives of House_n are the PlaceLAb and the Open Source Building Alliance. House_n develops, among other things, technologies and design strategies based on context aware sensors that transmit information on decision processes and acti-vities. The researchers are concentrating on three areas of application: health ("pro-active environments for a healthy lifestyle"), energy (strategies for zero-energy houses) and mass production (building components for living spaces). One of the projects of House_n looks at physical and digital systems that promote a healthy lifestyle at home and in public space. They developed and tested technologies in

Boston, for example, to motivate people to use a staircase rather than an elevator.

Hyperbody, TU Delft, NL
http://protospace.bk.tudelft.nl, www.hyper-bodyblog.com

Hyperbody ist eine Forschergruppe an der Architekturfakultät der Technischen Universität Delft unter Leitung von Prof. Kas Oosterhuis. Hyperbody zählt zu den Pionieren auf dem Forschungs- und Anwendungsgebiet inter-aktiver Architekturen. Hyperbody beschäftigt sich mit Fragen der Interaktivität nicht nur hin-sichtlich kollaborativer Entwurfsprozesse, sondern auch während der Nutzung und War-tung von Gebäuden. Hyperbody entwickelt neue Ideen und praktische Anwendungen inter-aktiver Architekturen und interessiert sich dabei für alle Phasen des Lebenszyklus von Gebäuden sowie für deren ökonomische und ökologische Konsequenzen. Aktuell arbeitet Oosterhuis mit seinen Kollegen etwa an einer interaktiven Wand als „emotivem Prototypen", also einer Wand mit „Gefühlen" für ihren Nutzer.

Hyperbody is a research group in the archi-tecture faculty of the Technical University Delft, directed by Prof. Kas Oosterhuis. Hyperbody is among the pioneers in the research and application of interactive architecture. Hyper-body examines questions of interactivity not only with respect to collaborative design pro-cesses, but also over the course of the use and maintenance of buildings. Hyperbody devel-ops new ideas and practical applications for interactive architectures and is interested here in all phases of the lifecycle of buildings as well as in their economic and ecological

consequences. Currently, for example, Oosterhuis is working with his colleagues on an interactive wall as an "emotive prototype"—a wall, that is, with "feelings" for its user.

Design Interactions, Royal College of Art, UK
www.interaction.rca.ac.uk/

Diese Abteilung des Londoner Royal College of Art fokussiert auf die Potenziale digitaler Technologien im Bereich Design. Darüber hinaus setzt sie sich mit der Verbindung von Design- und Bio- sowie Nanotechnologie auseinander. Geleitet wird die Abteilung von Anthonny Dunne vom Designerduo Dunne & Raby (siehe S. 52).

This department of the London Royal College of Art focuses on the potential of digital technologies for the area of design. They also examine the connection between design and biotechnology/nanotechnology. The departmend is directed by Anthony Dunne of the designer duo Dunne & Raby (see p. 52).

Weitere Ressourcen (Auswahl)
Additional Resources (Selection)

www.emanate.org

Die Non-Profit-Organisation „Materials & Applications" aus Los Angeles beschäftigt sich mit der Erforschung neuer Materialien und Technologien für den öffentlichen Raum.

The non-profit-organization "Materials & Applications" from Los Angeles is engaged in the exploration of new materials and technologies for public space.

www.interactivearchitecture.org

Blog und Projektsammlung zu interaktiver Architektur von Ruairi Glynn, UK.

Blog and collection of projects on interactive architecture by Ruairi Glynn, UK.

www.kitchenbudapest.hu

Media Lab für junge Forscher, gegründet 2007 in Budapest, das sich mit der Konvergenz mobiler Kommunikation, Onlinekommunikation und dem urbanen Raum beschäftigt.

Founded in 2007 in Budapest, the media lab for young researchers examines the convergence of mobile communication, online communication and urban space.

www.situatedtechnologies.net

„Situated Technologies: Toward the Sentient City" ist ein Kooperationsprojekt der Architectural League New York, dem Center for Virtual Architecture und dem Institute for Distributed Creativity. Im September 2009 wird unter anderem eine Ausstellung in New York präsentiert, die sich mit der Beziehung zwischen ubiquitous computing und Architektur im urbanen Raum auseinandersetzt. Im Rahmen dieses Vorhaben wird – neben anderen – auch das Projekt Natural Fuse von Usman Haque (siehe S. 142) realisiert.

"Situated Technologies: Toward the Sentient City" is a cooperation between the Architectural League New York, the Center

for Virtual Architecture, and the Institute for Distributed Creativity. In September 2009 they will present an exhibition in New York, dealing with the connection between ubiquitous computing and architecture in urban space. This will include a realization of–among others– the project Natural Fuse by Usman Haque (see p. 142).

http://robotecture.com/

Projekt- und Linksammlung zu interaktiver Architektur von Michael A. Fox, USA, Gründer der MIT Kinetic Design Group und Co-Autor von „Interactive Architecture", Princeton Architectural Press, 2009.

Collection of projects and links on inter- active architecture by Michael A. Fox, USA, founder of the MIT Kinetic Design Group and co-author of "Interactive Architecture," Princeton Architectural Press, 2009.

www.spatialrobots.com

Projekt- und Linksammlung zu räumlicher Interaktivität und neuen Technologien in der Architektur von Miles Kemp, USA, Co-Autor von „Interactive Architecture", Princeton Architectural Press, 2009.

Collection of projects and links on spatial interactivity and new technologies in archi- tecture by Miles Kemp, USA, co-author of "Interactive Architecture," Princeton Architectural Press, 2009.

Index

Kurzbiografien
Short Biographies

Bengt Sjölén (SE)

www.automata.se
Scattered House (S. / p. 30), Aleph (S. / p. 86)

Software- und Hardware-Designer aus Stockholm. Gründungspartner von Automata AB, Teenage Engineering AB, iPic System AB. Beteiligung an europaweiten Projekten, die Medienkunst, Technologie und Architektur zusammenführen und soziale und physische Räume erforschen. Internationale Ausstellungen, u.a. im ISEA (San Jose, USA, 2006 / Helsinki, 2004), Trondheim Senter for Samtidskunst (Trondheim) und Ludwig Muzeum (Budapest).

Software and hardware designer from Stockholm, founding partner of Automata AB, Teenage Engineering AB, iPic System AB. Participation in Europe wide projects, merging media art, technology and architecture experimenting with social and physical spaces. Internationally exhibited, e.g. at ISEA (San Jose, USA, 2006 / Helsinki, Finland, 2004), Trondheim Senter for Samtidskunst (Trondheim) and Ludwig Muzeum (Budapest)

Jason Bruges (UK)

www.jasonbruges.com
Wind to Light (S. / p. 108), Aeolian Tower (S. / p. 110)

Studium der Architektur an der Oxford Brookes University und am University College London, anschließend bei Foster and Partners und als Interaction Designer bei Imagination tätig. 2001 Gründung von Jason Bruges Studio, um maßgeschneiderte interaktive Installationen für unterschiedlichste Kunden herzustellen.

Study of architecture at Oxford Brookes University and University College London, before working at Foster and Partners and as an interaction designer at Imagination. Founding of Jason Bruges Studio in 2001 to create bespoke interactive installations for a diverse range of clients.

Carole Collet (UK)

www.carolecollet.com
Toile de Hackney (S. / p. 44), RemoteHome: Kinetic Wall (S. / p. 38)

Textil-Designerin und Beraterin für Textildruck, R&D, nachhaltiges Design und intelligente Textilien. Leiterin des Masterstudiengangs Textile Futures und Forscherin am Central Saint Martins College, Associate Director der Textile Futures Research Unit an der Universität der Künste in London. Ausstellungen u.a. im Science Museum und im Victoria & Albert Museum in London.

Textile-Designer and consultant in the area of textile print, R&D, sustainable design, and intelligent textiles. Course Director, MA Textile Futures and Researcher at Central Saint Martins College, Associate Director of the University of the Arts Textile Futures Research Unit. Exhibitions at the Science Museum and the Victoria & Albert Museum in London.

doubleNegatives Architecture (JP / HU / CH)

www.doublenegatives.jp / www.corpora.hu
Corpora in Si(gh)te (S. / p. 104)

Kollektiv aus Architekten und Künstlern, Gründung 1998 durch den Architekten Soto Ichikawa. Setzt sich mit Prozessen und Instrumenten zur Erfassung des Raumes als eigenständige Architektur auseinander. Ausstellungen u.a. im Yamaguchi Center for Arts and Media (YCAM), auf

der 11. Internationalen Architekturausstellung in Venedig 2008 und auf derTransmediale 2009 in Berlin.

Team of architects and artists, founded in 1998 by architect Sota Ichikawa. Assembles a new team for each projects and focuses on the processes and devices used to measure space as architecture. Exhibitions at Yamaguchi Center for Arts and Media (YCAM), the 11th international architecture exhibition in Venice 2008, andTransmediale 2009 in Berlin.

Dunne & Raby (UK)

www.dunneandraby.co.uk
Technological Dream Series: No. 1 Robots (S. / p. 52), Faraday Chair (S. / p. 58)

Anthony Dunne leitet den Fachbereich Interaction Design am Royal College of Art (RCA) in London. Studium in Industrial Design und PhD in Computer Related Design am sRCA. Gründungsmitglied des CRD Research Studio mit Fiona Raby. Fiona Raby studierte Architektur und Computer Related Design am RCA. Lehrtätigkeiten in Architektur und Design Interactions. Internationale Ausstellungen und Veröffentlichungen. Arbeiten von Dunne & Raby sind u.a. Teil der Sammlungen des MoMA, des Victoria & Albert Museums, Frac Ile-de-France und FNAC.

Anthony Dunne is head of the Design Interactions department at the Royal College of Art (RCA) in London. Study of Industrial Design and PhD in Computer Related Design at the RCA. Founding member of the CRD Research Studio, together with Fiano Raby. Fiona Raby studied architecture and Computer Related Design at the RCA. Teaching activities in architecture and Design Interactions.. International exhibitions and publications. Works of Dunne & Raby are part of the permanent collections such as MoMA, the Victoria & Albert Museum, Frac Ile-de-France and FNAC.

Franziska Eidner (GER)

Herausgeberin / editor

Kulturwissenschaftlerin und Kulturmanagerin aus Berlin. Konzeption und Kommunikation von Ausstellungen, Publikationen und Veranstaltungen im Architekturbereich. u. a. für das Deutsche Architektur Zentrums DAZ, den Bund Deutscher Architekten BDA und sally below cultural affairs. Gemeinsam mit Nadin Heinich und Nadine Jerchau Herausgeberin von „Überfunktion. Zur Konstruktion von Wirklichkeiten in der Architektur" (2007).

Cultural scientist and cultural manager, located in Berlin. Project development and communications for exhibitions, publications and events in the area of architecture, for the German Center for Architecture (DAZ), the Association of German Architects (BDA), sally below cultural affairs and others. Together with Nadin Heinich and Nadine Jerchau, she published "Hyperfunction. On the construction of realities in architecture" (2007).

Ruairi Glynn (UK)

www.interactivearchitecture.org
Performative Ecologies (S. / p. 132), Angels (S. / p. 136)

Interaction Design-Studium am Central Saint Martins College of Art and Design in London und am Institute of Digital Art and Technology in Plymouth, Studium der Architektur an der Bartlett School of Architecture in London. Tutor an der Bartlett School of Architecture und dem Central Saint Martins College of Art and Design. Entwicklung von Installationen für den öffentlichen Raum, Gründer des Online-Informationsportals www.interactive architecture.org.

Study of Interaction Design at Central Saint Martins College of Art and Design London, and at the Institute of Digital Art and Technology in Plymouth, study of architecture at the Bartlett School of Architecture in London. Tutor at Bartlett school of Architecture and at Central Saint Martins College of Art and Design. Production of public art installations, founder of the online resource www.interactivearchitecture.org.

G TECTS LLC (USA)

www.gtects.com
Harlem Mediatech (S. / p. 78), Baruch College (S. / p. 80)

1999 von Gordon Kipping in New York gegründet. Beschäftigt sich sowohl in konzeptionellen als auch gebauten Projekten mit der Beziehung zwischen elektronischer Informationstechnologien und Architektur. Gordon Kipping studierte Architektur an der University of Toronto und am Southern California Institute of Architecture. Adjunct Assistant Professor an der Columbia Universität.

Founded in 1999 by Gordon Kipping in New York. Pursues both conceptual projects and built work with a particular interest in exploring relationships between electronic information technologies and architecture Gordon Kipping: studied architecture at University of Toronto and Southern California Institute of Architecture. Adjunct Assistant Professor Columbia University.

Usman Haque

www.haque.co.uk / www.pachube.com
Reconfigurable House (S. / p. 26), Scattered House (S. / p. 30), Open Burble (S. / p. 124), Pachube (S. / p. 138), Natural Fuse (S. / p. 142)

Gründer von Haque Design + Research. Bis 2005 Dozent am Interactive Architecture Workshop an der Bartlett School of Architecture in London. Gastforscher am Interaction Design Institut in Ivrea, Italien, Artist-in-Residence an der Internationalen Akademie für Medienkunst und Wissenschaft in Japan. Internationale Ausstellungen und Auszeichnungen, u.a. Design of the Year Award (interactive) 2008 des Design Museums, UK.

Founder of Hacque Design + Research. Until 2005, teacher in the Interactive Architecture Workshop at the Bartlett School of Architecture, London. Invited researcher at the Interaction Design Institute Ivrea, Italy, artist-in-residence at the International Academy of Media Arts and Sciences. Internationally exhibited and awarded, e.g. Design of the Year Award (interactive) 2008 of the Design Musueum, UK.

HeHe (FR / UK / GER)

www.hehe.org
Grandes Lignes (S. / p. 94), Nuage Vert (S. / p. 106)

1999 von Helen Evans und Heiko Hansen gegründet. Internationale Ausstellungen und Auszeichnungen, u.a. mit dem Golden Nica und dem Prix Green For Environmental Art im Jahr 2008. Lehrtätigkeit u.a. am Interaction Design Institute Ivrea, ENSCI / Les Ateliers in Paris und an der Universität Amsterdam. Helen Evans studierte Technical Arts Design an der Wimbledon School of Art und Computer Related Design am RCA in London. Heiko Hansen studierte in Hamburg Maschinenbau (HAW) und Industriedesign (HFBK) sowie Computer Related Design am RCA in London.

Founded by Helen Evans and Heiko Hansen in 1999. Internationally exhibited and awared, including the Golden NICA and the Prix Green For Environmental Art in 2008. Teaching activities at the Interaction Design Institute Ivrea, The ENSCI / Les Ateliers in Paris and the University of Amsterdam. Helen Evens studied Technical Arts Design at the Wimbledon School of Art and Computer Related Design at the Royal College of Art (RCA) in London. Heiko Hansen studied Mechanical Engineering at the University of Science, Industrial Designs at the University of Arts in Hamburg, Germany and Computer Related Design at the RCA.

Nadin Heinich (GER)

www.plana-office.com
Herausgeberin / editor

Architekturvermittlerin und Kuratorin aus Berlin. Gründung von plan a noch während des Studiums als Projektplattform junger Kultur- und Architekturschaffender. Ausstellungs- und Publikationsprojekt „Überfunktion" in der Architekturgalerie Aedes Berlin (2007). Auszeichnung der Publikation „Überfunktion — Zur Konstruktion von Wirklichkeit(en) in der Architektur" (gemeinsam mit Franziska Eidner und Nadine Jerchau) mit dem Preis Schönste Bücher 2008 der Stiftung Buchkunst.

Curating and mediting of architecture. Based in Berlin. Founding of plan a during her studies. Exhibition and publication project "Hyperfunction" at gallery Aedes (Berlin) in 2007. The publication "Hyperfunction—On the construction of realities in architecture" (together with Franziska Eidner and Nadine Jerchau), was awarded with the prize Schönste Bücher 2008 (Most beautiful books) by the Stiftung Buchkunst.

Toyo Ito (JP)

www.toyo-ito.com
Tower of Winds (S. / p. 70)

Studium der Architektur an der Universität Tokio. Gründung von „Urban Robot" (1971) in Tokio. Umbenennung in Toyo Ito & Associates (1979). Gastprofessor an der Columbia Universität, Honararprofessor an der University of North London. Zahlreiche internationale Ausstellungen und Auszeichnungen, u.a. Goldener Preis des Japanese Good Design Award (2001), RIBA Royal Gold Medal (2005).

Study of architecture at Tokyo University. Founding of "Urban Robot" in Tokyo (1971), asince 1979 Toyo Ito & Associates. Guest professor at Columbia University and honorary professor at the University of North London. Numerous international exhibitions and awards including the Gold Prize of the Japanese Good Design Award in 2001 and the RIBA Golden Medal in 2005.

Judith Keller (GER)
www.judithkeller.com
Art Director

Studium der Visuellen Kommunikation an der Universität der Künste (UdK) in Berlin und am London College of Communication (LCC). Seit 2002 als Fotografin und Grafikerin in Berlin tätig, von 2006 bis 2007 Geschäftsführung Kreation bei der Studentischen Kommunikationsagentur Töchter + Söhne an der Universität der Künste Berlin. Künstlerische Leiterin der ausgezeichneten plan-a-Publikation „Überfunktion" (2007).

Study of Visual Communications at University of Arts (UdK) in Berlin and at London College of Communication (LCC). Since 2002 photographer and graphic designer in Berlin, from 2006 to 2007 managing director "creation" for the student communication agency Töchter + Söhne at University of the Arts in Berlin. Art Director of the awarded plan a publication "Hyperfunction" (2007).

Manolis Keladis (UK)
Otto (Madsounds) (S. / p. 48)

Designer und Ingenieur, beschäftigt sich aktuell mit der Zukunft des traditionellen Buchs als Interface um digitale Inhalte zugänglich zu machen. Dozent am Royal College of Art und Fellow an der Tanaka Business School des Imperial College London. Frühere Arbeiten reichen von der Gestaltung von Kunstausstellungen für Sony bis zu Forschungsarbeiten an der Eidgenössischen Technischen Hochschule (ETH) Zürich.

Designer and engineer, currently focussing on the future of the traditional book as an interface to access digital content. Lecturer at Royal College of Art and Fellow at Imperial College's Tanaka Business School in London. Previous works range from designing art exhibitions for Sony to researching at the Swiss Federal Institute of Technology ETH Zurich.

Erik Kirkortz (SE)
www.emotionalcities.com
Emotional Cities (S. / p. 92)

Studium der Bildenden Kunst an der Konstfrack–Universität für Kunst, Handwerk und Design in Stockholm und an der Universität der Künste in Berlin. Seit 2006 Arbeit an Projekten, die das Internet mit interaktiven Lichtinstallationen im öffentlichen Raum verbinden: Colour by Numbers (2006) in Zusammenarbeit mit Loove Broms und Milo Lavén, seit 2007 Emotional Cities.

Study at the department of fine art at Konstfack - the University college of Art, Crafts and Design in Stockholm and at the University of Arts in Berlin. Focuses on projects connecting the internet with interactive light installations in public spaces: Colour by Numbers (2006), a collaboration with Loove Broms and Milo Lavén, since 2007 Emotional Cities.

Karen Van Lengen (USA)
www.arch.virginia.edu
MIX House (S. / p. 50)

Architekturstudium am Vassar College und an der Columbia Universität. Edward E. Elson Professorin für Architektur und seit 1999 Dekanin der School of Architecture an der Universität Virginia. Tätigkeit als Design Associate bei Pei & Partners in New York City, danach Gründung des eigenen Büros KVL. Van Lengen war Vorsitzende des Fachbereichs für Architektur an der Parsons School of Design in New York, wo sie den renommierten Design Build Workshop etablierte.

Study of architecture at the Vassar College and the Columbia University. Edward E. Elson Professor of Architecture and Dean of the School of Architecture at the University of Virginia (since 1999). After working as a Design Associate for I. M. Pei & Partners, New York City, she founded her own studio KVL. Van Lengen chaired the Department of Architec-ture at Parsons School of Design in New York, where she founded the renowned Design Build Workshop.

J. MAYER H. (GER)

www.jmayerh.de

Housewarming MyHome (S. / p.46)

1996 in Berlin von Jürgen Mayer H. gegründet. Arbeiten an den Schnittstellen von Architektur, Kommunikation und Neuen Technologien. Aktuelle Projekte sind u.a. das Stadthaus im Scharnhauser Park in Ostfildern und Metropol Parasol - die Neugestaltung der Plaza de la Encarnacion in Sevilla. Jürgen Mayer H.: Architekturstudium an der Universität Stuttgart, The Cooper Union New York und an der Princeton University. Zahlreiche internationale Veröffentlichungen und Ausstellungen. Präsenz in Sammlungen wie dem MoMA NY und dem SF MoMA.

Founded in 1996 in Berlin by Jürgen Mayer H. Focus on works at the intersection of architecture, communication and new technology. Recent projects include the Town Hall in Ostfildern, Germany and the redevelopment of the Plaza de la Encarnacion in Sevilla, Spain. Jürgen Mayer H.: study of architecture at Stuttgart University, The Cooper Union and at Princeton Universtiy. Numerous international publications and exhibitions, part of international collections like the MoMA New York and SF MoMA.

Christian Moeller (US / GER)

www.christian-moeller.com

Mojo (S. / p. 96), Nosy (S. / p. 98)

Künstler und Professor an der Fakultät für Design / Media Arts an der Universität Kalifornien (ULCA) in Los Angeles. Studium der Architektur an der Fachhochschule in Frankfurt und an der Akademie der Bildenden Künste in Wien. 1990 Gründung eines eigenen Büros und Medienlabors in Frankfurt, bis 2001 Professor an der Staatlichen Hochschule für Design in Karlsruhe, seit dem in den USA lebend.

Artist and professor at the Department of Design / Media Arts, University of California (UCLA) in Los Angeles. Study of architecture at the College of Applied Sciences in Frankfurt and at the Academy of Fine Arts in Vienna. In 1990 he founded his own studio and media laboratory in Frankfurt. He was a professor at the State College of Design in Karlsruhe, Germany until he moved to the United States in 2001.

NOX– Lars Spuybroek (NL)

www.Noxarch.com

D-Tower (S. / p. 90)

Lars Spuybroek studierte Architektur an der Technischen Universität Delft und gründete das Architekturbüro NOX in Rotterdam. Herausgeber des Magazins NOX (später Forum). Zahlreiche Auszeichnungen und internationale Ausstellungen, u.a. auf Biennalen in Venedig, im Centre Pompidou in Paris und im Victoria & Albert in London. Seit 2001 Professor für Digitale Entwurfstechniken an der Universität Kassel. Seit 2006 außerordentlicher Professor und Ventulett Distinguished Chair für Architectural Design am Georgia Institute of Technology in Atlanta.

Lars Spuybroek studied at the Technical University in Delft and founded the architecture office NOX in Rotterdam. publisher of the magazine NOX (later Forum), Numerous awards and international exhibitions, e.g. at several Venice Biennales, the Centre Pompidou in Paris and the Victoria & Albert in London. Since 2001 professor of Digital Design Techniques at the University of Kassel in Germany. Since 2006 professor and Ventulett Distinguished Chair in Architectural Design at the Georgia Institute of Technology in Atlanta.

plan a (GER)

www.plana-office.com

Herausgeber / editor

plan a ist eine junge Architekturplattform, die von Nadin Heinich im Jahr 2004 initiiert wurde. Ziel ist es, als Impulsgeber und Katalysator zu einem zukunftsgerichteten Dialog über Architektur beizutragen. Insbesondere möchte plan a Positionen einer jungen Generation von Architekten vermitteln und ein erweitertes, interdisziplinäres Verständnis von Architektur und Umweltgestaltung forcieren.

plan a is a young architecture platform initiated by Nadin Heinich in 2004. It aims to contribute as promoter and catalyst to a future-directed dialogue on architecture. In particular, plan a wants to communicate the positions of a young generation of architects and force a broader, interdisciplinary understanding of architecture and environmental design.

Cedric Price (UK)

Fun Palace (S. / p. 114), Inter-Action Center (S. / p. 116)

Gilt seit „Fun Palace" (1960-72), das er zusammen mit der Theaterdirektorin Joan Littlewood entwickelte, als einer der innovativsten Architekten Großbritanniens. Studium der Architektur an der Cambridge Universität und an der Architectural Association (AA) in London. 1958 bis 1964 Lehrtätigkeit an der AA und am Council of Industrial Design. Herausgeber von „Non-plan" (1969, mit Sir Peter Hall und Paul Baker), Gründung von „Polypark" (1971), ein Netzwerk von Architekturhochschulen. Cedric Price starb 2003 in London.

Renown as one of the most architects in the UK since "Fun Palace" (1961-72), developed in association with the theatre director Joan Littlewood. Study of architecture at Cambridge University and at the Architectural Association (AA) in London. From 1958 to 1964, lectures at the AA and at the Council of Industrial Design. Publication of "Non-plan" (1969, with Sir Peter Hall and Paul Baker), founder of "Polypark" (1971), an architectural schools network. Cedric Price died 2003 in London.

realities:united (GER)

www.realities-united.de

A.AMP (S. / p. 72), UEC ILUMA (S. / p. 76)

Im Jahr 2000 von den Brüdern und Architekten Tim und Jan Edler in Berlin gegründet. Projekte in Europa, Asien und den USA; Kooperationen mit Architekten Coop Himmelb(l)au, Foster & Partners, Renzo Piano, Bjarke Ingels, MASS Studies und Nieto Sobejano. Zahlreiche Preise und internationale Ausstellungen, u.a. auf der Architekturbiennale in Venedig, im Vitra Design Museum, im Kunstmuseum Stuttgart und im Schweizer Architekturmuseum. Im Jahr 2009 Auszeichnung mit dem Förderungspreis der Akademie der Künste, Sektion Baukunst.

Founded in 2000 by the brothers and architects Tim and Jan Edler in Berlin. Projects in Europe, Asia and the United States; collaborations with Coop Himmelb(l)au, Foster & Partners, Renzo Piano, Bjarke Ingels, MASS Studies, Nieto Sobejano and others. Numerous awards and international exhibitions including the Venice Biennale for Architecture, the Vitra Design Museum, the Kunstmuseum Stuttgart and the Swiss Architecture Museum. In 2009, awarded with the Förderungspreis award in the category "architecture" from the Academy of the Arts Berlin.

Ben Rubin (USA)

www.earstudio.com

MIX House (S. / p. 50)

Medienkünstler und Leiter der Multimediafirma EAR Studios in New York City. Studium der Visual Studies an der Brown Universität und am Massachusetts Institute of Technology (MIT) Media Lab. Lehrtätigkeit an der Yale School of Art. Ausstellungen u.a. im Whitney Museum of American Art, MIT List Visual Arts Center und in der Brooklyn Academy of Music. Auszeichnung mit dem Golden Nica Preis von Ars Electronica 2004 und dem Webby Award 2003.

Media artist and director of the multimedia firm EAR Studios in New York City. Studied visual studies at Brown University and Massachusetts Institute of Technology (MIT) Media Lab. Teaches Yale School of Art. Exhibitions at the Whitney Museum of American Art, the MIT List Visual Arts Center and the Brooklyn Academy of Music. Awarded with the Golden Nica Prize from Ars Electronica 2004 and a Webby award in 2003.

Ken Sakamura (JP)

www.tronweb.super-nova.co.jp

TRON Intelligent House, PAPI (S. / p. 22)

Professor für Informatik an der Universität Tokio. Gründer des TRON-Projektes (The Real-time Operating system Nucleus), u.a. mit Anwendungen für den Architekturbereich. Seit 2006 Leiter des Ubiquitous Networking Laboratory (UNL) sowie des T-Engine Forum for Consumer Electronics. Mitglied in der Japan Information Processing Society (JIPS), dem Institute of Electronics, Information and Communications Engineers (IEICE), der Association for Computing Machinery (ACM) und dem Institute of Electrical and Electronics Engineers (IEEE). Auszeichnung mit dem Takeda Award for Social / Economic Well-Being 2001 (mit Richard Stallman und Linus Torvalds) sowie Preise des JIPS, IEICE und IEEE.

Professor in Informsation science at the University of Tokyo. Founder of the TRON Project (The Real-time Operating Nucleus) with applications also for architecture. Since 2006,

director of the ubiquitous networking laboratory (UNL) in Tokyo and of the T-Engine forum for consumer electronics. Member of the Japan Information Processing Society (JIPS); the Institute of Electronics,Information and Communications Engineers (IEICE); the Association for Computing Machinery (ACM); and the Institute of Electrical and Electronics Engineers (IEEE). Takeda Award for Social / Economic Well-Being (2001 with Richard Stallman and Linus Torvalds), several awards from JIPS, IEICE, and IEEE

Joel Sanders (USA)

www.joelsandersarchitect.com
MIX House (S. / p. 50)

Studium der Architektur an der Columbia Universität, Gründung des eigenen Architekurbüros JSA in New York City. Associate Professor für Architektur an der Yale Universität. Zuvor Lehrtätigkeiten an der Parson School of Design und der Princeton Universität. Herausgeber von „Stud: Architectures of Masculinity" (Princeton Architectural Press, 1996) und Autor für „Art Forum" und „Harvard Design Magazine".

Study of architecture at the Columbia University, founding of his own architecture studio JSA in New York City. Associate Professor of Architecture at Yale University. Before, teaching activities at Parsons School of Design and Princeton University. Editor of "Stud: Architectures of Masculinity" (Princeton Architectural Press, 1996), and author for "Art Forum" and "Harvard Design Magazine."

Tobi Schneidler (UK / GER)

www.tobi.net / www.maoworks.com
Remote Home (S. / p. 38), Robotic Furniture: Lonely Home Bench (S. / p. 42)

Studium der Architektur an der Architectural Association in London, Gründung von maoworks. Verschiedene anwendungsbezogene Forschungsprojekte im Bereich Tangible Media und interaktive Architektur. Lehrtätigkeiten u.a. am Royal College of Art in London und der Königlich Technischen Hochschule (KTH) in Stockholm. Ausstellungen u.a. im Institute of Contemporary Art, dem Victoria & Albert Museum, dem Pompidou Centre und dem SF MoMA.

Study of architecture at the Architectural Association in London, founder of maoworks. Various applied research projects within tangible media and interactive architecture. Teaching activities at e.g. the Royal College of Art in London and The Royal institute of Technology (KTH) in Stockholm. Exhibitions e.g. at the Institute of Contemporary Art, the Victoria & Albert Museum, the Pompidou Centre and SFMoMA.

Adam Somlai-Fischer (HU)

www.aether.hu
Reconfigurable House (S. / p. 26), Scattered House (S. / p. 30), Aleph (S. / p. 82)

Architekt und Interaction Designer. Studienabschluss des Architecture + Urban Research Laboratory an der Königlich Technischen Hochschule (KTH) in Stockholm. Lehrtätigkeiten in Architektur und Medientechnologie am KTH, Gastwissenschaftler im Smart Studio (heute Interactive Institute) Stockholm und am MOKK Media Research. Workshops in Design-Schulen wie der Domus Academy in Mailand und dem Goldsmith College in London. Gründer und Leiter von „aether architecture" in Budapest.

Architect and interaction designer. Graduation from the Architecture + Urban Research Laboratory at the Royal Institute of Technology (KTH) in Stockholm. Teaching activities in Architecture and Media Technology at KTH, guest researcher at the Smart Studio (now Interactive Institute) Stockholm, guest researcher at the MOKK Media Research. Workshops in design-schools such as Domus Academy, Milan and Goldsmith College, London. Founder and director of "aether architecture" in Budapest.

Mette Ramsgard Thomsen (DK)

www.cita.karch.dk
Slow Furl (S. / p. 126), Vivisection (S. / p. 130)

Architekturstudium an der Königlichen Akademie in Kopenhagen und der Barlett School of Architecture in London. Leiterin des CITA - Center for Information Technology and Architecture in Kopenhagen. Fokus auf die Entwicklung von „Mixed Realities", der Erfahrung von Räumen, die sowohl durch eine physische als auch eine virtuelle Dimension definiert sind. Gründung von Escape (2003 mit Jesper Mortensen). Workshops u.a. in Amsterdam, Barcelona, Seoul und Kopenhagen.

Study of architecture at the Royal Academy in Copenhagen and the Barlett School of Architecture in London. Head of CITA - Center for Information Technology and Architecture in Copenhagen, Denmark. Focus on the development of Mixed Realities, the experience of spaces which are defined by part physical part virtual dimensions. Co-founder of Escape (2003 with Jesper Mortensen). Workshops, e.g., in Amsterdam, Barcelona, Seoul and Copenhagen.

Duncan Wilson (UK)

www.duncan-wilson.com
Otto (Madsounds) (S. / p. 48)

Produktdesign-Studium an der Glasgow School of Art und Studium „Design Products" am Royal College of Art in London. Neil Morris Prize for Furniture 2001 für „stepchair", 2. Preis beim „New Walls, Please!" Competition 2004 für „Pixel Notes Wallpaper" (in Zusammenarbeit mit Sirkka Hammer). Seit 2007 als Produktdesigner für BarberOsgerby in London tätig.

Study of Product Design Glasgow School of Art and Design Products at the Royal college of Art in London. Neil Morris Prize for Furniture 2001 for "stepchair", 2nd Prize at the "New Walls, Please!" competition 2004 for "Pixel Notes Wallpaper" (in collaboration with Sirkka Hammer). Since 2007 product designer for BarberOsgerby in London.

Credits

Alle als Collageelemente verwendeten Fotografien / All photos used as elements in the collages: Judith Keller

TRON Intelligent House Abbildungen / images: Ken Sakamura
PAPI - Toyota Dream Home *Abbildungen* / images: Ken Sakamura. Entwickelt in Zusammenarbeit mit / developed in collaboration with Toyota Home, Inc.
Reconfigurable House *Abbildungen* / images: Adam Somlai-Fischer. Team: Usman Haque, An Haque, Ai Hasegawa, Barbara Jasinowicz, Gabor Papp, Bengt Sjölén, Adam Somlai-Fischer, Tamas Szakal
Scattered House Abbildungen / images: Adam Somlai-Fischer. Team: Usman Haque, Bengt Sjölén, Adam Somlai-Fischer, Agoson Nagy (stc), Barbara Jasinowicz, Andras Szalai, Zsolt Korai, Tamas Bagi, Nitipak Dot Samsen, Annita Koutsonanou
RemoteHome Abbildungen / images: Tobi Schneidler / maoworks. Team: Tobi Schneidler, Adam Somlai-Fischer, Frederik Petersson, Carole Collet, Loove Broms, Stefanie Schneidler. Unterstützt durch / supported by: The Interactive Institute, Smart Studio (SE)
Robotic Furniture Abbildungen / images: Tobi Schneidler / maoworks. Team: Tobi Schneidler, Loove Broms, Milo Lavén. Unterstützt durch / supported by: Victoria & Albert Museum London
Toile de Hackney Abbildungen / images: Carole Collet. Designer: Carole Collet, electronic engineer: Jon Sawdon Smith, textile technicians: Kevin Bolger, Arantza Vilas Sarasua, Design Laboratory at Central Saint Martins College. Unterstützt durch / supported by: Research department, Central Saint Martins College of Art and Design, University of the Arts, London
Housewarming MyHome Abbildungen / images: J. Mayer H. / Thomas Dix (Fotograf / Photographer). Team: Jürgen Mayer H., Jonathan Busse, Marcus Blum
Otto (Madsounds) Abbildungen / images: Duncan Wilson Team: Duncan Wilson, Manolis Kelaidis (IDE, Royal College of Art) Ausgestellt auf der / Exhibited at IDE Performance Show, 2006
Mix House sAbbildungen / images: Joel Sanders, Karen Van Lengen, Ben Rubin. Team: Ben Rubin / EAR Studio, Joel Sanders / JSA, and Karen Van Lengen / KVLA... Entwickelt für / Developed for „Open House: Intelligent Living by Design", Vitra Design Museum, Weil am Rhein / Art Center College of Design, Pasadena
Technological Dream Series: No. 1 Robots Abbildungen / images: Dunne & Raby. In Auftrag gegeben von / curated and commissioned by: Jan Bolen, z33. Video: Noam Toran, Robot Sound Design: Scanner, Computer modelling: Graeme Findlay
Faraday Chair Abbildungen / images: Dunne & Raby
Tower of Winds Abbildungen / images: Toyo Ito & Associates / Shinkenchikusha (Fotograf / Photographer)
A.Amp Abbildungen / images: realities:united. In Zusammenarbeit mit / in collaboration with: WOHA Architects. Team (realU): Johann Christoph Bätz, Jan Edler, Tim Edler, Wolfgang Metschan, Daniel Mock, Malte Niedringhaus, Stefan Tietke, Christoph Wagner, Markus Wiedauer
UEC ILUMA Abbildungen / images: realities:united. In Zusammenarbeit mit / in collaboration with: WOHA Architects. Team (realU):

Malte Niedringhaus, Gunnar Krempin, Stefan Ludwig Neudecker, Markus Wiedauer, Christoph Witte, Jan Edler, Tim Edler, Daniel Mock
Harlem Mediatech, Baruch College Abbildungen / images: G TECTS
Aleph Abbildungen / images: Adam Somlai-Fischer. Team: Adam Somlai-Fischer, Bengt Sjölén
D-Tower Abbildungen / images : Lars Spuybroek. In Auftrag der Stadt / commissioned by the city of Doetinchem (NL). NOX Team: Lars Spuybroek, Pitupong Chaowakul, Chris Seung-woo Yoo, Norbert Palz. Künstler / Artist: Q.S Serafijn. V2_Lab: Simon de Bakker, Artem Baguinski
Emotional Cities Abbildungen / images: Erik Kirkortz. Lichtinstallationen Stockholm / Light installations Stockholm: Anders Örnberg, Anders Halling
Grandes Lignes Abbildungen / images : André Morin (S. / p. 94), alle anderen / all others: HeHe
Mojo Abbildungen / images: Anna Kwan. Ort / Location: 7th Street / Centre Street, Port of Los Angeles, San Pedro CA. Kurator / curator Marc Pally. Programmierung / programming: Sven Thoene. Herstellung / fabrication: Carlson & Co
Nosy Abbildungen / images: Christian Moeller. Ort / Location: Art Garden, Osaki City, Tokyo. Kurator / Curator: NANJO and ASSOCIATES, Tetsu Nagata
Corpora Insi(gh)te Abbildungen / images: dNA. Kernteam / core Team: Sota Ichikawa, Ákos Maróy, Max Rheiner, Kaoru Kobata
Nuage Vert Abbildungen / images: Niklas Sjöblom. Nuage Vert in Helsinki wurde präsentiert von / was presented by Pixelache Festival of Electronic Art and Subcultures.
Wind to Light Abbildungen / images: Jason Bruges Studio In Zusammenarbeit mit / in collaboration with: onedotzero, Light Lab
Aeolian Tower Abbildungen / images: Jason Bruges Studio. Präsentiert bei / Presented at One Dot Zero – adventure In Motion festival
Fun Palace, Inter-Action Centre Abbildungen / images: Cedric Price Fonds, Collection Centre Canadien d'Architecture / Canadian Centre for Architecture, Montréal
Open Burble Abbildungen / images: Usman Haque. Kernteam / core team: Usman Haque, Rolf Pixley, Kei Hasegawa, Fred Guttfield, Seth Garlock, Susan Haque, Ai Hasegawa
Slow Furl Abbildungen / images: Mark Bryant. Ausstellung / exhibition: The Lighthouse Gallery. Gefördert durch / Supported by Arts Council England, Lighthouse (Brighton), RIBA (Sussex Branch) u.a. / a.o.
Vivisection Abbildungen / images: Anders Ingvartsen. Ausstellung / exhibition: Charlottenborgs Efterårsudstilling, Robotic Membranes exhibition at Grand Parade Gallery, University of Brighton
Performative Ecologies, Angels Abbildungen / images: Ruairi Glynn
Pachube Abbildungen / images: Haque Design + Research. Team: Usman Haque, Sam Mulube, Chris Leung, Ai Hasegawa
Natural Fuse Abbildungen / images: Haque Design + Research Teil der Ausstellung / part of the exhibition „Situated Technologies: Toward the Sentient City". Unterstützt durch / supported by: The Architectural League of New York. Team: Usman Haque, Nitipak, Dot' Samsen, Cesar Harada, Barbara Jasinowicz, Ai Hasegawa